MW01401611

OCT 14	DATE DUE		
OCT 27			
FEB 13 1995			

305.42
LAN

Landau, Elaine
SEXUAL HARASSMENT

KAMLOOPS SEC. S. LIBRARY

Sexual Harassment

Sexual Harassment

Elaine Landau

Walker and Company
New York

Copyright © 1993 by Elaine Landau

All rights reserved. No part of this book may be reproduced or transmitted in any form or by any means, electronic or mechanical, including photocopying, recording, or by any information storage and retrieval system, without permission in writing from the Publisher.

First published in the United States of America in 1993 by Walker Publishing Company, Inc.

Published simultaneously in Canada by Thomas Allen & Son Canada, Limited, Markham, Ontario

Library of Congress Cataloging-in-Publication Data
Landau, Elaine.
Sexual harassment / by Elaine Landau.
p. cm.
Includes bibliographical references and index.
Summary: Examines the varied forms that sexual harassment can take, discusses instances of harassment in both work and school settings, and offers suggestions on how to handle such situations.
ISBN 0-8027-8265-5. —ISBN 0-8027-8266-3 (lib. bdg.)
1. Sexual harassment—United States—Juvenile literature.
[1. Sexual harassment.] I. Title.
HQ1237.S48   1993
305.42—dc20   92-43748
CIP
AC

Text Design: Susan Phillips

Printed in the United States of America

2 4 6 8 10 9 7 5 3 1

For Susan Graver

Contents

1. Sexual Harassment   *1*
2. Thomas/Hill: Someone Is Not Telling the Truth   *12*
3. The Cost of Sexual Harassment   *26*
4. Sexual Harassment in Schools   *41*
5. What You Can Do   *60*

APPENDIX 1. Employee Rights Legislation   *69*

APPENDIX 2. Equal Employment Opportunity Offices   *71*

APPENDIX 3. Organizations Concerned with Sexual Harassment and Related Issues   *77*

For More Information   *81*

Source Notes   *85*

Index   *89*

Sexual Harassment

1
Sexual Harassment

*F*or as long as she could remember, Penny Muck had been enchanted with the music business. As a young girl living in Texas, she frequently stayed after school to help the music teachers, hoping one day to pursue a career in the highly competitive pop music industry. When years later she moved to Los Angeles and landed a job at prestigious Geffen Records, whose recording artists included Cher, Aerosmith, and Guns N' Roses, it was as if a lifelong dream had come true.

Muck ambitiously looked forward to a bright career with the record company. She was intelligent and hardworking, and seemed to have a natural flair for the business. When she began her job in September 1988 she got along well enough with her supervisor, Mark Babineau, but after he was promoted to general manager of a new Geffen label things changed.

Refusing to relate to Muck as a professional any longer, Babineau began making obscene remarks and gestures to her. In response, she once fled from the room, while on other occasions she'd try to reason with him or even scold him for his inappropriate behavior. As she explained in an interview for television, "I'd say things to Mr. Babineau like, 'You know, you're really sick. You need to get some help.' And he would look me straight in the face, put up his fists, and go, 'You know, this is a good sickness, though. You should catch this.'"[1]

In the months that followed, Penny Muck did her best to skirt around her boss's unwarranted advances. She had a well-paying job she wanted to keep, and she didn't want her position at Geffen jeopardized. Muck tried to make sure that she wasn't alone with Babineau and that their interactions remained as brief as possible. But by July of that year she realized that her supervisor wasn't going to allow her to continue evading him. One afternoon he unexpectedly cornered her in his office, unzipped his pants, and began masturbating. At that moment Penny Muck knew for certain that her dream job in the recording industry had turned into a nightmare: she was being sexually harassed.

Muck was not alone in her plight. Just the previous year a group of women on RCA's record staff reported having been sexually harassed by a senior vice president while at an out-of-town music conference. And when a young woman named Laurie Harris worked as an assistant to Mike Bone, president of Island Records—recording label for the rock group U2—her experience was similar. Bone made a pass at Harris, and when she refused his overtures he became extremely hostile. Although she thought he would probably apologize the next day for what he'd done, that didn't happen.

"I never got, you know, remorse," she explained. "I never got anything like that. I got aloofness, I got arrogance. That's what I got. And I got fired, that's what I got."[2] Mike Bone, on the other hand, later became president of an even larger record label.

Individuals working in related industries are frequently subjected to the same type of abuse. One high-powered attorney representing a number of music superstars is known to have sexually harassed several of his secretaries. In one instance, after insisting that a young woman take dictation in his bedroom, he emerged naked from the adjoining bathroom.

The female attorneys he employed were also subjected to unwarranted advances. One woman arrived at her boss's home for what she believed was a business meeting, only to find him waiting for her barely dressed. He immediately suggested that the firm's business would improve if she went away for a weekend with one of his major clients.

Increased reports of sexual harassment within the record community reveal that women in the industry are frequently treated that way. Many of the men they work with view it as a natural consequence of the circumstances. Some may even feel that the women are there for their amusement and entertainment. As a member of the popular band Van Halen put it, "Can you blame them? Look, they hire these fine secretaries and then they harass them."[3]

Yet the roots of sexual harassment are much deeper. While inappropriate sexual advances obviously reflect the problem on one level, sexual harassment is actually not about sex—it's about power and its abuse. This abuse is especially prevalent in male-dominated industries, where a woman's career can be instantly destroyed if it's even rumored that she's a troublemaker or uncooperative.

Abby Liebman of the California Women's Law Center, a policy group for women's issues, described the widespread existence of sexual harassment in the pop music industry: "It's a business where everybody wants to be there, everybody wants to get ahead. It's very attractive. There's a sense that you're expendable, that you can be more easily intimidated in that kind of environment. And in that kind of milieu you're going to find sexual harassment."[4]

However, sexual harassment can affect members of nearly any industry: doctors, lawyers, typists, construction workers, journalists, librarians—even members of Congress. In many ways, sexual harassment may have become an inherent aspect of the American workplace. A *Newsweek* poll indicated that 21 percent of the women surveyed had been sexually harassed on their jobs, while an additional 42 percent knew someone who had been harassed. Other surveys reflect that about half of all American women have experienced sexual harassment at one time or another while in the work force.

Although there are documented incidents of men being

sexually harassed by women, these are significantly fewer in number. Filed complaints of homosexual and lesbian harassment are comparably rare, although some labor experts estimate that this may actually occur far more frequently than is known. A sexual harassment counselor who placed a newspaper ad offering confidential counseling for same-sex harassment was surprised to receive over twenty inquiries within a two-week period. One homosexual harassment case that recently captured the nation's attention involved the World Wrestling Federation. A twenty-one-year-old man claimed that while working for the Federation as a teenage ring assistant, he was sexually harassed by both executives and front-office employees. Shortly thereafter a number of other young men in the industry supported his allegations, claiming that they'd been similarly treated.

Despite its prevalence in our society, at times there's been some confusion as to what precisely constitutes sexual harassment and what avenues for redress are available. Perhaps in its broadest sense, sexual harassment largely amounts to sexual pressure at school or work that a person is in a difficult position to refuse. This can span a wide spectrum of behaviors, ranging from obscene jokes to sexual assault. A person who is sexually harassed may be continually propositioned or flirted with while at work. Sexual harassment also encompasses staring at a woman's breasts while she is making a business presentation or looking up her skirt as she bends over at the file cabinet. "Men don't understand that caged feeling," noted University of Texas sociologist Susan Marshall. "But women know what sexual harassment is. It's when your hair stands up, when you feel like you're being stalked."[5]

Some social critics argue that, although sexual harassment can occur in any industry, it is especially prevalent in blue-collar industries where women are breaking into fields formerly dominated by men. "It's not just some guy grabbing you and pushing you into a closet and saying, I'm going to fire you," acknowledges feminist author Susan Faludi. "It's more the subtler form of making women feel uncomfortable by turning the workplace into a locker room and telling them, 'What's the matter, you can't handle it? You want equality; I'm going to give it to you with a vengeance.' . . . It's a slow, relentless accumulation of slights and insults that add up to the same thing—the message that we don't want you here and we are going to make your hours here uncomfortable."[6]

This analysis is strongly supported by statistics. In industries where women comprise less than a quarter of the work force, the number of sexual harassment complaints amounts to about two per one thousand females. But in situations where over half the employees are women, the complaint drops to less than half that number. "Pioneers are often vulnerable," one sexual harassment counselor noted in reviewing the numbers, "whether it's the first woman police officer [on a force] or the first woman neurosurgeon [at a hospital]."[7]

In recent years, the slew of lawsuits launched by sexually harassed individuals—combined with the pressure for American companies to formulate comprehensive guidelines—has underscored the need for new legal precedents to handle these situations. Much of what is legally regarded as sexual harassment today has evolved through a number of significant court decisions. While earlier sexual harassment cases were heard in court, a breakthrough case occurred in 1977, when the Court of Appeals in the District of Columbia found that a woman named Paulette Barnes was a victim of discrimination. Barnes's government job was abolished following her refusal to have sex with her supervisor. In its decision the Court of Appeals established sexual harassment as a form of sexual discrimination, which is illegal under Title VII of the Civil Rights Act of 1964.

The illegality of sexual harassment as well as its scope were later noted in another landmark ruling. In 1986 the United States Supreme Court found in favor of a Washington bank teller, Mechelle Vinson, who sued both her supervisor and company for sexual harassment. During the trial it was revealed that Vinson's supervisor had fondled her in front of other employees, followed her into the rest room, and even raped her on several occasions. The court's judgment in this case was especially significant since it specified that, in addition to blatant forms of harassment such as those Vinson had endured, a sexually "hostile environment" at the workplace also constitutes sexual harassment.

Since that time other court rulings have widened the boundaries of sexual harassment. In January 1991 a Florida federal court determined that displaying nude pictures on bulletin boards or walls at work is a form of sexual harassment. Just a few days later in San Francisco, a three-judge panel ruled that, as men and women often view things differently, the overriding factor in determining whether an individual has been sexually harassed is whether a "reasonable woman" might feel threatened by the situation. In this case an IRS worker who'd refused to date one of her coworkers continued to receive unwelcome love letters from him. As one of the justices presiding over the case wrote, "Men, who are rarely victims of sexual assault, may view sexual conduct in a vacuum without a full appreciation of the underlying threat of violence that a woman may perceive."

Unfortunately, sexual harassment has long been a reality for women in situations extending far beyond the workplace. In early 1991 thirteen women living in the same apartment building won an eight-hundred-thousand-dollar judgment against their landlord for continuing to employ a building manager who had sexually harassed many of the female tenants. Court records indicate that despite their protests the building manager had frequently grabbed the women's bodies. Those who fell behind in their rent were told that they either had to pay up immediately or model flimsy lingerie for him. Since all the harassed women were single mothers of limited financial means, many felt especially vulnerable to his threats.

Some feminists argue that since sexual harassment is so

pervasive, such behavior needs to be recognized and stopped at once. However, strict regulation of the extremely common and widespread practices that constitute sexual harassment would be difficult to achieve. For example, many women might agree that at times obscene comments made to them by men on the street can be threatening. Yet it is unrealistic to think that there's always going to be a law enforcement officer nearby to arrest the offenders. Most women just end up trying to walk away as quickly as possible. As Boston University professor Frances Grossman puts it, "From the guys who work on the street to the biology professor who tells a sexist joke in class, to the guy who says, 'Hey baby, let's go out,' to the guy who rapes—all these are part of a piece in their role of disempowering women. Men say these are not related behaviors. Flirting and jokes are fine, and rape is bad, they say. But increasingly, sociologists say they all send the same disempower-message to women."[8]

The practical difficulties in pursuing sexual harassment cases have stopped many women from righting this wrong. While the number of sexual harassment cases reported to the Equal Employment Opportunity Commission (EEOC—the federal agency that investigates harassment incidents in the workplace) has risen in recent years, attorneys as well as many women's groups claim that these numbers represent only a tiny fraction of the actual occurrences. This may be because women are often either unaware of their rights or afraid to exercise them. As a representative from the California Women's Law Center describes the situation, "Women are subjected to a barrage of sexual innuendo, pictures and verbal abuse, and most don't have the vaguest idea that they don't have to put up with it."[9]

Women workers who take their cases to court face considerable obstacles. It is often very difficult for a woman to undermine a man's denial. Experienced sexual harassment attorneys feel that it generally takes the testimony of at least three credible women before a judge will even question whether a man refuting the charges against him is telling the truth.

In addition, these trials tend to be time-consuming, emotionally draining, and financially unrewarding. Under the Civil Rights Act of 1964, courts were only authorized to award women back pay. There were no provisions for the punitive damages that plaintiffs in other cases could win, even though sexually harassed women are often fired or feel forced to leave their jobs. While some women have won substantial judgments in sexual harassment cases in states with their own antiharassment laws, these are few and far between. Instead, sexually harassed women generally pay rather high legal fees to get their day in court. Since sexual harassment cases tend to be difficult to win, and even then result in low settlements, many attorneys demand high fees, which often have to be at least partially paid by the woman beforehand.

Even attorneys such as Patricia J. Barry, who won the 1986 precedent-setting case before the Supreme Court involving Washington State bank teller Mechelle Vinson, have found the plight of women wishing to sue difficult and complex. After finally filing for bankruptcy in 1988, Barry announced that she was going to give up civil rights suits in favor of divorce and child custody work. Barry pinpointed the inherent problems in sexual harassment trials: "Most judges perceive themselves as identifying with the man no matter how horrible he is. It becomes [a case of] the woman versus the man."[10]

Perhaps this attitude was especially evident in the case of Karen Kouri, a Virginia shipping firm employee who sued when her boss continued to send her greeting cards and gifts and insist on walking her to her car and the rest room, as well as rubbing her back. When the case went to court the male judge rejected Kouri's claim of harassment, stating that Kouri's supervisor had not insisted that she have sex with him. The judge also blamed the woman for what had occurred, claiming that Kouri sent out "mixed signals" by not forcefully telling her supervisor to stop his offensive behavior, and that "the harassment in this case was not unwelcome."

Feminist organizations insist that the values of a male-dominated society were even more apparent when a New York appeals court overturned a four-million-dollar punitive damage award for sexual harassment won by *Penthouse* model Marjorie Thoresen. The forty-one-year-old model claimed that she'd been coerced into having sex with two of the publisher's business associates in order to keep her job. Once again, the legal system squarely placed the blame on the harassed woman. One of the justices who heard the case openly criticized women who pursue careers in the sex industry and seek damages for sexual harassment afterward. As he noted in the court decision, "Whatever exploitation occurred here was self-exploitation, willingly undertaken for monetary and other gain."[11]

Many feminists were outraged by what they perceived as the court's gender-based morality, along with its outdated, male-oriented view of women. Perhaps Ellen B. Holtzman, president of the Women's Bar Association of the State of New York, best summed up their feelings in response to the court's ruling: "Any opinion from the bench which indicates 'She got what she deserved' is demeaning and sends a message to society that sexual misconduct in the workplace is justified under certain circumstances. It is not."[12]

Although women's rights still need to be elevated within the court system, an important stride was made with the passage of the Civil Rights Act of 1991. While the former civil rights law prohibited sexually harassed individuals from collecting punitive damages, the new act affords them an opportunity to do so. The legislation still does not go as far as some feminists would wish, however, since it sets limitations on the amounts awarded in accordance with a company's size. On a sliding scale, a sexually harassed person may only win up to $50,000 from a company with fifteen to one hundred workers, or up to $300,000 from concerns employing five hundred or more people.

Sexually harassed women in a few states, such as California and Texas, that have their own antiharassment laws may be best off ignoring the new federal law and suing in state court, where there are no limits on the damage awards. Still, for those without state legal protection, the new act significantly enhances their position. Besides allowing sexually harassed individuals to collect damages, the Civil Rights Act of 1991 entitles them to jury trials, which tend to yield more sympathetic verdicts than judges' rulings. The new law also permits the judge to require the losing party to pay the winner's expert-witness fees. Expert witnesses, who can attest to the detrimental effects of sexual harassment on a woman, frequently prove crucial to the case. But sexually harassed women have often been unable to afford the service of these professionals.

Despite these steps forward, there are still serious problems associated with bringing sexual harassment cases to court. Prior to suing the party in question, in most states those wishing to bring sexual harassment complaints must first file them with the U.S. Equal Employment Opportunity Commission or another area-designated fair employment agency. These agencies are frequently backlogged with an overload of cases—it may take the EEOC as long as eight months just to process a new case. Usually the agency will try to work out a settlement between the parties involved prior to resorting to legal alternatives. But despite intervention by an outside government agency, sexually harassed employees frequently find that their companies are reluctant to arrive at a settlement. For example, in 1990 only about 40 percent of the concerns charged with sexual harassment were willing to settle, and even in these cases the compensation offered tended to be low.

Although the EEOC itself is empowered to bring a case to court, it tends not to do so. Of about sixty thousand employee discrimination cases received by the agency in 1990, just 640 lawsuits were initiated. Now that under the new civil rights law damages may be awarded, however, some sexually harassed employees are requesting a "right-to-sue" letter from the agency and hiring their own lawyers to bring these actions to court. A right-to-sue letter from the EEOC simply means that the agency will not initiate a lawsuit on the woman's behalf. This document indicates whether or not the commission believes the abuse actually occurred; even if the agency finds the complaint invalid, however, an individual still has the right to go to court to prove her case.

While winning a sexual harassment case may now yield greater monetary rewards, sexually harassed individuals still often experience difficulty finding competent legal representation. In spite of recent legal changes, these cases are still considered tough to win. Many attorneys believe that the courts must work out a more precise definition of sexual harassment; catchphrases such as "hostile environment" and "reasonable woman," they feel, are too general to be genuinely useful, and in some instances may actually work against a sexually harassed individual. These lawyers insist that better guidelines as to precisely what constitutes an unwarranted and inappropriate act in the workplace are needed to solidify sexual harassment charges.

As these issues are ironed out, some legal experts expect to see changes in the new civil rights legislation itself. They've argued that the ceiling on damages awarded in accordance with company size should be removed, as it's unconstitutional to limit awards for one class of citizens and not another. Once this provision is challenged in court, we may find that the Civil Rights Act of 1991 is just the start of new legal restraints against sexual harassment in the United States.

2
Thomas/Hill: Someone Is Not Telling the Truth

*A*lthough sexual harassment in one form or another has existed for as long as anyone can remember, the issue was thrust to the forefront of the nation's consciousness in the fall of 1991. Judge Clarence Thomas had been nominated to the United States Supreme Court. During the Senate Judiciary Committee's confirmation hearings, Thomas was accused of sexually harassing a female staff member who had formerly worked under him. The assertion came as a shocking revelation to both Washington, D.C., politicians and the rest of the country. Even those in opposition to Thomas's conservative views found it difficult to reconcile such assertions with the judge's reputation for integrity.

Thomas's coworkers painted a portrait of the judge as a paragon of politeness and sensitivity to women. No sooner were the accusations leveled at him than a number of women who had also previously worked with Thomas rushed to his defense. For example, Doris Rozzi, director of the Office of Federal Operations at the EEOC, had been Clarence Thomas's subordinate for seven years. She described her former supervisor as the epitome of refinement, mentioning that she'd never even seen Thomas listen to an off-color joke, let alone tell one. "People thought he was a little uptight and conservative," she stated. "The word was, 'You have to go to Clarence with clean hands.'" Janet Brown, a former colleague of Thomas's, publicly acknowledged that when she'd been sexually harassed and had confided in Thomas, she found him exceptionally attuned to her predicament. As Brown added, "Outside of my immediate family, there was no one who exhibited more compassion, more outrage, more sensitivity and more caring than Clarence Thomas."[1]

Friends and classmates at Thomas's alma mater, Holy Cross College in Worcester, Massachusetts, agreed that Clarence had demonstrated exceptional sensitivity to women's rights and issues before it became fashionable to do so. As an undergraduate, the judge urged his campus's Black Student Union to design guidelines regulating the conduct of men in dormitories permitting female weekend guests. "He was acutely aware of these things," a fellow student recalled, "when many of us weren't even thinking about them."[2]

Some who attended law school with Thomas seriously doubted whether he'd be preoccupied with pornographic films, as his accuser implied. While at Yale Law School a student in his morning study group described Thomas's attitude toward one such film: "We were all laughing hysterically. He was talking about how absurd it was."[3]

On the other hand, those who believed the charges hurled against Thomas during the Senate hearings found it especially ironic that he had formerly headed the EEOC—the government agency charged with safeguarding workers from this form of abuse. While some argued that it had been a case of the fox guarding the henhouse, Thomas's supporters stressed that he had persistently urged the Justice Department to back the EEOC's sexual harassment guidelines in its arguments before the Supreme Court.

Anita Hill, the thirty-five-year-old law professor who claimed that Clarence Thomas had sexually harassed her while he was her supervisor, was also well known for her upstanding character and integrity. Raised in an Oklahoma Baptist family of modest means, Hill learned early on the value of education and religion. After graduating as valedictorian of her high school class, Anita Hill majored in psychology at Oklahoma State University, where she distinguished herself as an outstanding student. She went on to attend Yale Law School on an NAACP scholarship. Throughout her school years Hill was never seen by her classmates as frivolous, but was generally regarded as a serious and dedicated young woman with a bright future.

After graduating from law school with honors in 1980, Hill spent a year working in private practice in Washington, D.C., before becoming Clarence Thomas's special assistant at the Department of Education's office for civil rights. One staff member who worked with both Hill and Thomas while Hill was employed there noted that "She [Hill] was a real straight arrow, very proper and straight laced. She was certainly no bimbo."[4] When Clarence Thomas later headed the Equal Employment Opportunity Commission (EEOC), Anita Hill became his special assistant there. To the surprise of some of her colleagues, however, she left her job after only a year to accept a position teaching law at Oral Roberts University. She later became a law professor at the University of Oklahoma, specializing in commercial law.

Before Anita Hill's allegations against Clarence Thomas surfaced, his ascent to the Supreme Court seemed certain. Although President Bush's team knew that liberal Democrats would not care for Thomas's conservative views, this exceedingly intelligent African-American man, who'd risen from poverty to prominence in political circles, appeared to have a scandal-free past.

Then in August of 1990 Nan Aron, head of the Alliance for Justice, a group opposed to Thomas's nomination, received a call from a male Yale Law School graduate who'd heard that the Supreme Court nominee had sexually harassed a former employee named Anita Hill. Before long members of several Senate staffs approached Hill to learn if there was any truth to the rumor. When first questioned, Hill was reluctant to speak about what had transpired, but she eventually agreed to relate her experiences to the Senate Committee to, as she said, "remove my responsibility" and "take the matter out of my hands."

Anita Hill initially requested that her identity remain confidential. There was even some speculation that she had hoped to make her charges known solely to the committee, so that Thomas could be quietly persuaded to withdraw as a Supreme Court nominee if it found her accusations credible. But a congressional staffer informed Hill that an allegation against a nominee cannot be circulated throughout the committee without the accused individual being given an opportunity to defend himself. Even though a witness confirming her story contacted the Senate shortly thereafter, Hill was again reminded that the committee's hands were tied until the nominee could be confronted.

While Hill noted that she'd "made a great effort to make sure it did not come to this," she finally agreed to publicly state her allegations. As she explained, "I felt I had to tell the truth. I could not keep silent."[5]

Thus Hill came to testify before the Senate Judiciary Committee. Surrounded by bright lights and television cameras, she related her version of what happened between Clarence Thomas and herself. In addition to the audience of senators and the media present, millions of viewers throughout the world also heard and evaluated her testimony, transfixed by their television sets as this very personal and often humiliating drama unfolded.

Cool and composed, yet maintaining a cooperative demeanor, Anita Hill looked directly at the committee while telling her story and responding to the senators' probing questions. She described her interactions with Clarence Thomas while he was her supervisor in government positions from 1981 to 1983, stating that Thomas had repeatedly asked her out and that, each time she refused, he had deliberately brought up sexual topics in the course of their workday. If her recollections were on target, there could be little doubt that the judge who now sought a permanent appointment to the highest court in the land was guilty of blatant sexual harassment.

"He'd talk about pornographic materials depicting individuals with large penises or large breasts involved in various sexual acts," Hill stated. "On other occasions he referred to the size of his penis as being larger than normal and he also spoke on some occasions of the pleasures he had given to women with oral sex." Hill further told how Clarence Thomas "spoke about acts that he had seen in pornographic films involving such matters as women having sex with animals, and films showing group sex or rape scenes." She added that "on several occasions Thomas told me graphically of his own sexual prowess."

Perhaps one of the most unsettling moments in Hill's testimony came as she related how the judge had picked up a can of Coke in her presence and asked, "Who has put pubic hair on my Coke?" She also recounted an incident in which Thomas alluded to a pornographic film star named Long Dong Silver, who supposedly had an unusually large sex organ. Eventually, Hill became so upset by her supervisor's inappropriate sexual explicitness that she was hospitalized due to "stress on the job."[6]

During the proceedings Hill was asked why she waited ten years to make these charges, as well as why she continued to work for Thomas once he moved from the Department of Education to the EEOC in 1982. Replying, "I'm embarrassed I didn't say anything," Professor Hill went on to explain that at the time she was young and vulnerable and hadn't wanted to do anything that might jeopardize her career prospects. She also stated that, since the harassment had abated for a time, she felt that it was safe to take the position under Thomas at the EEOC. However, Anita Hill remarked that on her last day at the job "he [Thomas] made a comment I vividly remember. He said that if I ever told of his behavior, that it would ruin his career."[7]

When questioned about her motives for speaking out, Hill stressed that she wouldn't have aired the charges against Thomas at all if she hadn't been approached by Senate Committee staffers. She soberly explained, "I have nothing to gain here. This has been disruptive of my life and I've taken a number of personal risks." Hill noted that she'd been threatened, although she did not elaborate on the nature or source of the intimidation tactics. She added, "I have [just] come forward and did what I felt I had an obligation to do."

Anita Hill proved to be an effective and moving witness. She answered the senators' questions without wavering or hesitation. Her words painted a vivid image of what it was like to experience sexual harassment, conveying all the pain, vulnerability, and humiliation that accompany the experience. Despite the time lapse between the events she described and her testimony, Hill's account was rich with consistent and vivid details, which awakened the sensibilities of millions who heard her. As law professor Judith Resnick of the University of California commented, "You're seeing a paradigm of a sexual-harassment case."[8]

Clarence Thomas vehemently denied Hill's charges. Feeling that his past had already been thoroughly scrutinized by the committee throughout the confirmation hearings, Thomas angrily retorted, "I would like to start by saying unequivocally, uncategorically, that I deny each and every single allegation against me today. . . . I am incapable of proving the negative. It did not occur."

In what at first sounded like a withdrawal from the Supreme Court nomination, Clarence Thomas flatly stated, "No job is worth what I have been through. No horror in my life has been so debilitating. Confirm me if you want. Don't confirm me if you are so led . . . I will not provide the rope for my own lynching. These are the most intimate parts of my privacy, and they will remain just that, private." As it turned out, Thomas had no intention of withdrawing, but was determined to clear his name. In his testimony at the Senate hearing the following day he stated, "I would have preferred an assassin's bullet to this kind of living hell," but insisted that he would "rather die than withdraw."[9]

The battle lines between Clarence Thomas and Anita Hill were clearly drawn. With contrasting stories and no witnesses to verify their interaction, the matter largely boiled down to a case of she said/he said. It was now up to the Senate voting on Thomas's nomination—and, to some extent, the country—to determine who was telling the truth.

In many ways Anita Hill had become a symbol for every woman who'd ever been harassed and degraded by a male supervisor or coworker who could significantly influence her career. Yet despite the recognition Hill's story evoked in numerous women, it was immediately apparent that her charges would be met by many with disbelief and disdain.

Feminists suggested that part of the problem lay with the investigatory panel—all male senators—who found it difficult fully to comprehend Hill's reactions and experiences. There was also the partisan aspect of the panel's questioning: while Republican senators supportive of the President's Supreme Court nominee brutally grilled Anita Hill, their Democratic counterparts failed to respond to Thomas in the same manner.

One savvy political analyst described the subsequent imbalance: "The asymmetry was tough to watch. The Democrats have always been the defenders of women's issues, but when one of those issues was brought to center stage, they caviled. Hill was savaged for three days by Republicans who played to win. No one cross-examined Thomas in the same tone."[10]

Having uncovered a phone log showing that Professor Hill called Clarence Thomas a number of times after leaving EEOC, the Republicans on the Senate investigatory panel asked her why she kept in touch with a man who harassed her. In response, Anita Hill explained that she didn't feel threatened by Clarence Thomas once he was no longer her supervisor, and, further, that her calls were all work-related. Republican senator Arlen Specter of Pennsylvania, who perhaps launched the most vigorous attack against Hill, questioned the validity of Hill's recollections eight to ten years following the episodes. But Hill asked the committee to look at the incidents in their totality: "If you start to look at each individual problem, then you won't be satisfied that it's true.

But the statement has to be taken as a whole. There is no motivation to show I'd make up something like this."[11]

Senator Specter also strongly insinuated that Anita Hill might be mentally unstable and had merely imagined the obscene comments she'd attributed to Thomas. In support of this theory he introduced an affidavit by an attorney named John Doggett, who'd been a Yale classmate of Clarence Thomas and a Washington, D.C., acquaintance of Anita Hill.

Doggett alleged that, while he was attending a going-away party for Hill at EEOC, she'd taken him aside and scolded him for not following through on what she'd interpreted as his romantic interest in her. Doggett felt that Hill's remarks that night had been "totally unfounded" and that he was left "feeling that she was somewhat unstable, and that, in my case, she fantasized about my being interested in her romantically." Anita Hill contested Doggett's statements, noting that she hardly knew him and that "I did not at any time have any fantasy about romance with him." Meanwhile women's groups across the nation lamented how an American woman can come forth in good faith to level accusations of sexual harassment, only to find that she's become the accused.

Witnesses also testified on Professor Hill's behalf. These included friends she'd previously confided in about the harassment as well as character witnesses who portrayed her as an intelligent, hardworking, levelheaded woman. Among those who stood by Hill throughout the Senate hearing were her family and her associates at the University of Oklahoma's College of Law. As one of Hill's fellow law professors described their feelings, "Every faculty member here believes in Anita's integrity and honesty. She's a good, sincere human being."[12]

Despite the impressive case Anita Hill presented, in the end Clarence Thomas won the heated debate that had taken center stage in the Senate Caucus Room. In a fifty-two to forty-eight vote, the lowest margin in this century, Thomas was confirmed as a justice of the Supreme Court. Although

Hill certainly amassed her share of supporters, the bulk of the public's empathy may have ultimately gone to Judge Thomas.

Some argued that the sway of sympathy toward Thomas was largely due to timing. As Anita Hill testified during business hours, when many Americans were at work, her emotionally charged personal appeal was missed by most of the people who heard Clarence Thomas's testimony during prime time. Perhaps University of Southern California law professor Susan Estrich best summed up the circumstances when she said, "Anita Hill spoke to five million Americans during the day, Thomas spoke to thirty million that night."[13]

However, feminist organizations across the country placed much of the blame squarely on the all-white, mostly male U.S. Senate, which some described during the proceedings as functioning very much like an exclusive men's club. With only two female senators, most of these men don't generally work with women as equals. Instead, they often receive star treatment from the women surrounding them. An orientation session for congressional spouses has even included instructions for successfully living with a celebrity. Former Missouri lieutenant governor Harriet Woods put it bluntly: "Senators prey on women as if they were groupies."[14]

This may be largely because Congress has exempted itself from most antidiscrimination laws. The only recourse available to a sexually harassed congressional staff member is to bring the matter before Congress's ethics committees, which have been notoriously lax in handling such cases. When in 1989 Representative Jim Bates of California admitted making lewd remarks to and inappropriately touching female staff members, he was leniently dealt with; the House Ethics Committee merely issued a letter of reproach to Bates, declining to take further action.

Regardless of their educational background or previous job history, female Senate staffers tend to have servile duties. In the course of a day's work they may be expected to stop by a congressman's house to pick up a change of clothes for him or go to a department store to exchange a gift he purchased for his wife. Female staffers are frequently asked to act as hostesses for their bosses, showing guest constituents or contributors around the premises as needed. On one occasion a female assistant delivering documents to her boss was asked to remove her jacket to enable the constituent with him to better view her figure.

It is not difficult to see why some senators, functioning as they do in this environment day after day, were not terribly upset by the sexual remarks Clarence Thomas was alleged to have made to Anita Hill. An aide to one of the senators of the Judiciary Committee described the predicament faced by women who work for these men: "You know what the code is, and if you want to be involved, you know what you have to tolerate. It's happened to me, and I never call anyone on it. You have to show that you are tough enough to take a certain kind of harassment."[15]

Regardless of the factors involved, many American women were outraged by what they perceived as the Senate's inability to comprehend vital women's issues as demonstrated by Clarence Thomas's Supreme Court appointment. Following the Thomas/Hill debate a Gallup poll indicated that roughly one out of every two people who viewed a substantial portion of the inquiry came away feeling less confident about Congress and the congressional process. The subsequent anger and dissatisfaction became even more evident through the protest staged by women in major cities throughout the nation. In a message directed at incumbents seeking reelection the following year, the protesters chanted "We'll remember in November."

Some social analysts described the outcry following the hearing as a feminist rebirth. Regardless of how the impetus was labeled, women of varying ages and backgrounds continued to target those senators who put Thomas on the Supreme Court. "Women made a difference in electing the Democratic Senate, particularly the Southern Democrats," a feminist spokesperson asserted. "Women have been the most loyal of Democratic voters. We gave them our votes. We gave them our money. And they gave us Clarence Thomas. We're fed up."[16]

Their visible protest included jamming the phone lines to the Democratic Party's national headquarters with angry calls regarding Thomas's appointment, as well as making donations to women's political organizations promising change. Due to the votes to affirm Judge Thomas by some Democratic senators, the Democratic Senatorial Campaign Committee, which strives to elect party members to the Senate, was dropped by its fund-raising agency. Women were known to have been among the committee's most generous and consistent supporters.

Patricia Ireland, executive vice president of the National Organization for Women, told the press, "We will no longer beg for our rights from men in power. We will replace them and take power ourselves." The Senate's confirmation of Thomas had a galvanizing effect on American women, which was further acknowledged by Fund of the Feminist Majority president Eleanor Smeal when she stated, "The Senate did more in one week to underscore the critical need for women in the Senate than feminists have been able to do in twenty-five years."[17]

The 1990s indeed appears to be the decade of women affecting government; some argue, however, that this political change might already have been underway. As of 1992 more women had run for political office, donated to political campaigns, and voted as a bloc than ever before. A 1992 *U.S. News & World Report* poll demonstrated that 80 percent of American women under thirty years of age believe the country would be more effectively governed if more women were in political office. Just eight years earlier, only 28 percent of women within the same age category had expressed that view.[18] This trend may at least be partly motivated by the compounding importance of such current women's issues as day-care, abortion, and, most recently, sexual harassment.

Females may also more easily ascend to public office due

to a phenomenon among male incumbents known as DIRE. DIRE—Death, Indictment, Retirement, Redistricting, and Exploitation—has already taken a visible toll on the careers of many elected male officials. By the time Clarence Thomas took his place on the Supreme Court, over fifty seats in Congress were open to newcomers, and more are expected to be available in the near future. The likely effect on Washington's political scene was perhaps best predicted by a GOP consultant: "Women will get a fairer shake."[19]

The Anita Hill/Clarence Thomas incident spurred set designer Eliza Townsend to run for the Maine state legislature. "I have never been so angry in my life," Townsend announced following Thomas's Supreme Court appointment. "Like most women, the hearing made me think about every nasty remark ever made to me. It was never so clear—women have to get involved."

As women's groups throughout the country had promised, the Senate's shabby treatment of Anita Hill also proved to be immediately problematic for a number of male politicians. It was cited as a major factor in former attorney general Richard Thornburgh's 1991 Senate race defeat. Senator Arlen Specter's relentless cross-examination of Professor Hill made things more difficult for him as well. Shortly after the hearings, while Specter campaigned for the Republican re-election primary, civic activist Lynn Yeakel, whose ad campaign featured Specter grilling Hill from the podium, campaigned for the Democratic nomination for the same Senate seat.

Women's political organizations have heavily relied on the Hill/Thomas episode as an effective fund-raising issue. The Women's Campaign Fund, which assists both Republican and Democratic women running for office, described the hearings as a "sickening spectacle" and used the slogan "This one's for Anita!" to encourage contributors to donate generously. By March 1991, contributions had doubled those given within the same period the previous year. Another political organization that funds only Democratic female candidates has tripled its membership since Clarence Thomas was placed on the Supreme Court. A 1992 press poll also indicated that half of the women in the country, as well as a third of the men, felt that the Senate confirmation hearings would have a bearing on their presidential vote that year.

Many of those who respected Anita Hill's courage in coming forward wondered how she'd fare after her public ordeal. Their anxiety was justified: following the hearings, Republican State Representative Leonard E. Sullivan of Oklahoma City suggested that Professor Hill be dismissed from her tenured post at the University of Oklahoma for having accused Judge Thomas of sexual harassment. Sullivan even offered to "buy out or otherwise remove Professor Hill from the campus and hopefully . . . [the] state."[20]

In many circles, however, Anita Hill was treated with respect and admiration. When addressing several hundred female state legislators only weeks after the Senate hearings, her enthusiastic audience twirled hundreds of pink napkins and pounded the table for several minutes as the young law professor entered the room. Describing sexual harassment as both "a form of violence against women" and an unrelenting "form of economic coercion," Hill urged women to reject inappropriate sexual behavior in the workplace.

"We are angry because we have been betrayed," Hill explained to the audience. "The reality is that this powerful [weapon] is used to reinforce a sense of inequality to keep women in their place, notwithstanding our increasing numbers in the workplace. We are angry because we have so little positive outlet for this anger."[21]

As she spoke, Hill's audience appeared energized by her message. Frequently interrupted by cheers and applause, Anita Hill advised the women to "seize their rage and resentment and turn it into positive energy." At one point during the evening someone asked Hill about the correct pronunciation of "harassment." But the astute law professor merely pointed out that regardless of how the word is pronounced, our lives will dramatically improve when we can "once and for all" simply "pronounce it dead."

Although sexual harassment is far from over in America, a number of trends surfaced following Anita Hill's emergence as a feminist figure. It may be noteworthy that attorneys in various parts of the country have reported an increased number of inquiries regarding possible cases. Sexual harassment training videos have also become essential basics in the personnel departments of many large corporations. Similar tapes designed to enhance sensitivity to the problem are being shown in some high schools and colleges as well.

Perhaps even more interesting is the effect Professor Hill's charges have had on work environments in other countries. Japan formerly regarded sexual harassment as more of a joke than a serious social issue. In fact, a number of Japanese bars had even been named "sekuhara"—"sexual harassment" in Japanese. When the Anita Hill/Clarence Thomas conflict made international headlines, the Japanese press ran editorials advising Japanese concerns with American plants and outlets to be aware of the problem. There was little genuine concern over sexual harassment in the Japanese workplace, but things may be changing.

In April 1992 a court in Fukuoka, Japan, shocked the public by finding in favor of a thirty-four-year-old woman who'd been sexually harassed by her supervisor at the small publishing company where she worked. Although her boss hadn't physically touched her, she felt forced to resign due to his persistent suggestive remarks. After the court awarded the woman $12,500 in damages, the Japanese business community began to take note of what might be a warning of things to come.

The verdict was also an important victory for Japan's newly born feminist movement, which had frequently referred to Anita Hill in describing the sexually harassed woman's plight. Anita Hill has become an important role model for women everywhere; it may still be too early, nevertheless, to assess the ultimate changes generated by the Oklahoma woman who challenged the establishment in speaking out against sexual harassment.

3
The Cost of Sexual Harassment

In 1987 thirty-five-year-old Patricia Kidd secured a position in Washington, D.C., organizing employee office space. Initially she did well and enjoyed her job, but before long her boss began making sexual advances toward her. Kidd tried to rebuff him, but he was not about to give up. Her supervisor's lewd remarks and indecent propositions continued.

Kidd, a divorced mother of two and the sole support of her family, pleaded with him to leave her alone. When her boss refused to take no for an answer she found herself waking up with a horrible knot in her stomach. The distraught woman went to the personnel office to request a transfer, but was told that her supervisor had to approve the move, which he'd already refused to do.

As time passed, Patricia Kidd's supervisor continued to insist that she have sex with him. On a number of occasions he threatened to have her fired if she didn't cooperate. He began calling Patricia at home asking if he could come over, but she'd always make up an excuse to keep him away. One morning after arriving at her job, Kidd noticed that her supervisor hadn't come in. A few hours later he called her at work, telling her to meet him at a nearby motel. When she hung up he called back moments later, warning Kidd that she could lose her job unless she complied.

Knowing that she couldn't afford to be out of work, Patricia gave in to him. She went to the motel, where she found her boss waiting for her in his bathrobe. Kidd later described their subsequent sexual encounter as "violent" and "demeaning." She said that she left feeling so "filthy" and depressed by the experience that she knew she could never do it again. When she later refused her boss's continued sexual demands, he retaliated with a vengeance. Her computer and support staff were reassigned, while Kidd was deliberately excluded from important departmental meetings she had attended in the past.

By May 1988 Patricia Kidd felt that she had to do something to change things. She described her predicament to her boss's supervisor, but he was unsympathetic, suggesting only that she try to improve her attitude. His reaction left Patricia feeling that her world was closing in on her, and soon afterward the situation began to affect her health. Subjected to the unrelenting stress, Kidd developed an ulcer and her hair began to fall out in large clumps.

Feeling that no one in a position of authority at work would assist her, Patricia Kidd took matters into her own hands and hired an attorney. She sued both her boss and his supervisors; despite the offenders' denials, a jury found in Kidd's favor. Yet even though she had won the case, in many ways Patricia Kidd felt as if she'd lost a great deal. Rehashing the details in court was painful, and the substantial legal fees she owed sometimes seemed insurmountable. Kidd also had to wait a considerable amount of time for the award's payment details to be worked out with the court.

The man who harassed Patricia Kidd retired following the trial, but his supervisors, who were also involved in the suit, remained on the job. After the trial, friends of the offender would still glare at Kidd when she saw them at work. Kidd longed for her life to return to normal; at times she'd just close the door and cry. Having been sexually harassed had taken a high personal toll on her.

Whether or not a sexually harassed woman goes to court, the stress and anxiety evoked by the experience is bound to negatively affect her. According to Wendy Crisp, director of the National Association for Female Executives, the largest women's professional association in the country, "This is not automatically a male-female issue. We define this issue as economic intimidation."[1] In addition to having to perform their assigned professional tasks, these women must also deal with either the stress of fending off their harasser or the shame and rage frequently associated with giving in to him.

Many women tolerate sexual harassment because they know that speaking out might cost them their careers. Females who report such abuses are frequently perceived as being "difficult" and are barred from climbing the rungs of the company ladder with any real degree of success. "A woman will complain and then becomes a pariah," explained a New York female attorney whose specialty is antibias cases. "If the male is in any way sanctioned, his male cohorts come to his defense and the woman becomes the wrongdoer and she's frozen out."[2]

At times even strong professional women have overlooked sexual harassment, fearing that as soon as they complain there'll be fifty other qualified individuals waiting in the wings to replace them. Women may frequently also have mixed feelings about confronting powerful mentors who've assisted them professionally in the past and could possibly influence their careers in the future. As a former manager of a California high-tech firm described when asked why she didn't speak out over twenty years ago when she was sexually harassed on the job: "I was a kid. I was trying hard to succeed. I told myself that this is the time to work hard, to jump through hoops, not the time to be spitting in people's faces and saying, 'I won't put up with this.' "[3]

Rather than receiving sympathy for the ordeal they've endured, women who file sexual harassment charges are usually more likely to find themselves subjected to intense scrutiny and criticism. Even women who've performed well at their jobs for years may now feel especially pressured to once again demonstrate their competence.

Many sexually harassed women experience negative consequences that continue for years to come. That's what happened to Lindsay Browne-Allison and Melissa Clerkin, two former California police officers. Both women had been subjected to seemingly endless forms of harassment at their jobs. Clerkin was called a lesbian and found a penis-shaped vibrator placed in her patrol car. Male officers frequently spoke graphically about sex in front of Browne-Allison and urinated outdoors in her presence.

The women sued the police department for sexual harassment. Although they won, their experience still had a negative effect on their lives and future. Lindsay Browne-Allison took a stress-related disability leave from her job and contemplated giving up her law enforcement career to study photography. "I won my case, but lost my career," she said. "Fighting this led to a divorce and made it practically and emotionally impossible for me to ever be a police officer again." Melissa Clerkin, who left the police department as well, stressed that although two women's lives were dramatically altered by their ordeal, the case appeared to have had little effect on the men who'd harassed them. She added, "All the same officers are still working there and haven't received any discipline. For them it's all just a big joke."[4]

The mental and emotional consequences of sexual harassment nearly drove a female officer to suicide in still another case. Cheryl Gomez-Preston had decided on a career in law enforcement as a young girl, and although at times training at the police academy had been difficult, she never considered giving up. Later on, as an academy graduate, Cheryl viewed her first position with the department as an opportunity to prove herself. She knew that as an African-American woman invading a male-dominated work realm, she would have difficulties to overcome, but she was determined to succeed. While initially some male officers hesitated to work with a woman, Cheryl eventually won them over and proved herself an able and valued member of the force.

Gomez-Preston worked at the precinct for about five years before marrying a young man attending medical school, whom she'd known since childhood. Things continued to go well for the policewoman until in 1982 she was transferred to the city's largest precinct. There Cheryl encountered a significant amount of ill will from some sexist officers, who also felt that Gomez-Preston didn't really need the job since she'd married a doctor. She received hostile and threatening phone calls replete with obscenities or racially charged phrases such as "Go back to Africa."

Upset over the situation, Gomez-Preston complained to her commanding officer, who also happened to be African-American. But her supervisor only made excuses for the other officers' unacceptable conduct and steered the conversation to a discussion of Gomez-Preston's personal life. He asked her if she was happily married and added that he liked her and wanted to have a personal relationship with her. Feeling extremely uneasy about the situation, Cheryl told her commanding officer that she was very happy at home and left the room.

Thinking that now she had nowhere to turn, Gomez-Preston began to feel increasingly isolated at work. After several of the officers learned that she hired a housekeeper to care for her children, Cheryl was accused of being snooty. Her coworkers' jealousy and negativity eventually placed the policewoman in a treacherous position; she felt that she wasn't always provided with adequate backup on dangerous assignments. The job Cheryl had once loved seemed to be disintegrating.

To remedy the situation, Gomez-Preston eventually filed a formal sexual harassment complaint against her commanding officer with the department's internal affairs division. Although her charges were supposed to initially remain confidential, word of what she'd done leaked out and Cheryl was transferred back to her original precinct. Now she found, however, that the warmth and acceptance she had once enjoyed there had evaporated, and many of the men had turned against her because of the action she'd taken against a fellow officer.

The tremendous stress she was under began to affect Cheryl Gomez-Preston's physical well-being. She had trouble sleeping and experienced frequent crying bouts. Her hair began to thin, and she stopped menstruating as well. Gomez-Preston became extremely depressed and at times had chest pains and blackouts.

Unable to find any relief in what she perceived as a no-win situation, Cheryl felt as though she'd hit rock bottom. One day while home alone she took out her handgun and held it to her temple. Tears streamed down her cheeks as she contemplated ending her pain forever. But when she thought about leaving her two young children without a mother, she couldn't go through with it. Knowing that she needed help, she checked herself into a hospital for six weeks.

There Cheryl Gomez-Preston finally received the support and understanding lacking at her job. She became convinced that she was not at fault, but had merely been in a high-stress situation with few available relief routes. Gomez-Preston also realized that she'd been rendered incapable of adequately functioning at work due to her supervisor's lack of assistance and his sexual overtures to her.

Still emotionally unable to return to police work, Cheryl Gomez-Preston sued the city's police force for sexual harassment. She began her suit on May 5, 1984, and finally won the case in April 1987. The jury awarded her $675,000 — at that time one of the largest sexual harassment judgments ever afforded a policewoman. Gomez-Preston also founded ASH — the Association for the Sexually Harassed — to assist both women and men who find themselves in the same position she did.

Instances of sexual harassment can have disastrous effects on everyone involved. That's what happened in a case involving a top investment firm's high-ranking partner and his secretary. Both professionally and personally, the man accused of sexual harassment here had seemingly achieved a level of success that most people only dream of. In addition to his renown in the investment world, he was a well-respected family man who'd won awards for his philanthropic fundraising. He traveled in prestigious business and political circles and the financial press had even hinted that he might be selected for a Washington, D.C., appointment.

His life and the lives of his family members would never be the same, however, after he was charged with sexual harassment by his assistant/secretary Kathy Abraham. Both Abraham and her supervisor admit that a romantic relationship between them had begun a number of years before, when her boss invited Kathy out for drinks along with several colleagues. The two later went to dinner and in time became embroiled in an affair.

After a while the situation soured for Abraham. She increasingly felt that she had to meet with her supervisor to please him and that it was becoming less a matter of her own free will. According to Kathy, "If I said I didn't want to meet him, he would become enraged and my life at the office that day would be intolerable. . . . I felt humiliated and I was humiliated."[5] She also felt especially degraded by his suggestion that she have sex with another of the firm's partners.

Abraham claims that she wanted the relationship to end but that her boss insisted it continue. Afraid of losing her position at the firm, she went along with his desires. Her attorney later described the situation: "This was total intimidation of a woman afraid for her job. A woman alone in an entry-level position with a child to support [Abraham was divorced]. A woman who had worked her way up, after many years, to $40,000 and a bonus. What was she going to do—go someplace and start over at half the salary?"[6]

Abraham was particularly upset when the unwanted liaison began to interfere with her duties at work. She stated that her boss insisted that she spend more and more time in his office discussing non-work-related matters. When Kathy informed him that she was falling behind in her work, he said he'd arrange for her to have less to do. "I had accounts, responsibilities. I dealt with customers," she said. "But then, slowly, he took it all away. He'd say 'Kathy is overworked; why don't we give this to someone else?' Someone else got my accounts, so he could sit and occupy my time. I was so frantic about my work and falling behind. I used to come in Sundays and drag my daughter with me, to try to catch up because that day he wouldn't be around."[7]

Although his attorney denied it, Abraham contends that her boss had a private telephone line temporarily installed so that he could call her directly from his desk without being listened in on or interrupted. "He would ask me certain questions and I was supposed to say certain things back to him. While everybody else was working, and I was supposed to be working, I had to sit and have sex conversations with him on this phone."

Kathy Abraham was tired of the situation, but saw no immediate alternative to her distasteful predicament. "I ask myself now, 'How could I let this happen?'" she asserted. "But I know why. I would have done anything to keep my job. Period. That's it. I had school fees to pay. I'd already put years in the company. I knew my check would come every two weeks, and there would be a bonus in December. Whatever else, I knew I could live this way."[8] She added that while at times her supervisor told her how fortunate she was that he loved and protected her, on other occasions he'd tell her "you can be replaced" and discuss other women at work to whom he was attracted.

After the involvement with her boss had continued for about four years, Abraham met a young New York City police officer at her synagogue, with whom she fell in love. At that point she told her boss that the sexual aspect of their relationship simply had to end. He became incensed and pressured Abraham to go out with him again, as well as continually questioned her about her new boyfriend. After nearly two months of intense harassment, she gave in to her boss's demands.

When her boyfriend learned the identity of the man she'd been afraid to break off with, he decided to confront the Wall Street financial wizard face-to-face, with Kathy present. But within minutes the meeting disintegrated into an insulting shouting match. Kathy accused her supervisor of sexually harassing her, while he defended himself, stressing that he'd never forced her to do anything. He also later claimed that she and her boyfriend had attempted to extort money from him through "outrageous allegations, destructive publicity, and lawsuits."

By now Abraham felt that she couldn't continue working for her boss, and was delighted when she was finally promised the transfer she'd hoped for. She, along with four other women at the firm, were to be promoted to the same new level together. But Abraham soon realized that her problems weren't over yet; in the months prior to her transfer, her supervisor still harassed her. Feeling that he'd never leave her alone as long as she worked for the company, she filed a criminal harassment complaint against him with the city police.

Soon afterward Abraham met with the firm's vice chairman, who informed her that the company was prepared to offer her a generous financial settlement to drop the complaint and leave the company. However, she was more interested in obtaining the upcoming promotion she'd been slated for. Just as she was about to start in her new position, someone leaked Abraham's charges regarding her former supervisor's unseemly behavior to the press. The conservative financial firm, obviously embarrassed by the adverse publicity, put both Abraham and her boss on leaves of absence.

Abraham's attorney noted that it seemed to be "the end of the line" for her client at the firm. While the attorney sought promises of job security and compensation for the damages Abraham had suffered, negotiations quickly broke down. By then Abraham was also not overly enthusiastic about her future job prospects, saying, "I've been told that as far as my type of work is concerned, forget it—I'm blacklisted on Wall Street."

Her supervisor also left the company; it was rumored that he was pressured into resigning and wasn't offered a limited partnership, as partners frequently are upon their departure. It was also thought that the early charges of extortion he had leveled at both Kathy and her boyfriend may have led to problems at the police officer's job as well. Regardless of what their futures may hold, the incident was costly for all three.

While ongoing abuse occurs in many areas of service and business, numerous industries have recently become more sensitive to its consequences due to the substantial sums of money courts have awarded sexually harassed individuals under the new civil rights bill and some state laws. After suing a Des Moines, Iowa, insurance company for sexual harassment, for example, Linda Monohan was awarded $1.3 million dollars for lost wages and emotional distress.

Monohan had started as a secretary at the company and eventually rose through the ranks to become a high-level broker. In 1979 three of her colleagues left to start their own firm and invited Monohan to join them as a vice president. She agreed, and although her new salary was less than that of the male partners in comparable positions, she didn't make an issue of it, claiming that she wasn't a feminist and was not about to rock the boat. For a time Monohan dated a fellow executive who'd also joined the new concern, but in the early 1980s she broke off their relationship. The man she'd been seeing did not want it to end and sometimes still left love notes on her desk.

In 1983 Monohan decided that she wanted to have a child and became pregnant. Although her former boyfriend was not the baby's father, he still wanted to marry Linda. She refused, emphatically stating that their romance was over.

Monohan had her baby in 1984 and, following her maternity leave, returned to work to find that there'd been some management changes at the company. The man she'd previously dated had been made her new supervisor, and before long Monohan realized that she wouldn't be permitted to function at her job as she had in the past. Now her boss excluded her from essential business meetings, interfered in her client relationships, and even threatened her with dismissal. Monohan complained to the company president, but left the firm after her claims of harassment were ignored. When the business later fought her right to receive unemployment benefits on the grounds that she had not been fired but had left voluntarily, Linda sued them in court for sexual harassment.

During the trial other female employees testified that the same supervisor had sexually harassed them. There were descriptive accounts of how he tore off strips of adding-machine paper to compare them to his penis length. The man in question even admitted touching one woman's breasts, claiming that he had misunderstood her body language.

Numerous other companies throughout the country have also already felt the financial sting of sexual harassment. In fact, by the late 1980s female staff members had filed sexual harassment complaints at 90 percent of the nation's largest corporations, and over a third of these companies had been previously sued for similar offenses. In addition to upheld court judgments, a recent survey of Fortune 500 companies revealed that sexual harassment costs such corporations as much as $6.7 million a year in absenteeism, turnover, and lost productivity—a figure that does not include additional millions in possible court costs and executive time. Besides these expenses, highly publicized sexual harassment cases can damage a company's reputation with the general public.

In response, some public and private employers have devised sexual harassment policies instructing their staffs in correct office etiquette. Such changes have often been instituted simply because it is good business to do so: Management teams reason that if a content work force is a more productive one, it is to their advantage to try to eliminate sexual harassment.

"No one is asking the company to solve society's problem," a workers' advocate explained. "The company is required to provide a safe, equal opportunity environment for men and women. The company has no right to change . . . [a man's] mind. What he thinks about women and sex is his business. But his behavior at the work place is the company's business."[9]

Many large corporations now frequently regard an equal opportunity employment director and support staff as essential, since courts can hold a company liable for sexual harassment occurring on its premises whether or not management was aware of it. Lawyers frequently advise their corporate clients that it's in the firm's best interest to give sexual harassment complaints their prompt attention. As one such attorney stated, "Given the liability that a company can incur if it doesn't protect the secretary who complains that her boss is harassing her, those interests are one and the same."[10]

At times sexual harassment may stem from a lack of understanding precisely what constitutes proper conduct at work. "I sometimes think we haven't touched the real issue," a human resources director of a large Chicago-based corporation noted. "I sense that there continues to be a need for management and employees to really understand what sexual harassment is. . . . There is still a lot of confusion over the subject. . . . It's hard for some men to realize that what they might get away with in a singles' bar or other social situations isn't acceptable behavior in the business environment. . . . I blame it on the lack of education and training at the corporation. It's a hard lesson to learn. Men still think sexual harassment is a joking matter."[11]

To remedy the situation, some companies have developed staff training sessions that utilize both video and classroom instruction, emphasizing that all employees need to be treated with dignity and respect. They stress that unbusinesslike conduct that might be construed as offensive or intimidating is unacceptable at the workplace. A number of national corporations offer annual seminars on sexual harassment for management-level staff, while lower-level employees learn about the company policy through distributed written materials that include a copy of the firm's code of conduct. Depending on the circumstances, violators may either be fired or sent for counseling.

One company known for its outstanding sensitivity in this area is Corning, Inc., in upstate New York. The practice of hiring female strippers for company birthdays had been abandoned there years ago, and by 1988 the organization required upper-level staff members to attend a two-day course promoting gender diversity and worker rights. Intensive orientation programs for all salaried staff teach employees to detect and curb racism, sexism, and sexual harassment.

AT&T has taken a similar stand to protect its staff. The corporation's written policy against sexual harassment incudes, but is not limited to, the following offensive behaviors: "unwelcome flirtatious advances, propositions, continual or repeated verbal abuse of a sexual nature, graphic verbal commentaries about an individual's body, sexually degrading words to describe an individual, and the display in the workplace of sexually suggestive objects or pictures." The policy also specifies that "no supervisor shall threaten to insinuate either explicitly or inexplicitly, that an employee's submission to or rejection of sexual advances will in any way influence any personnel decision regarding that employee's employment, wages, advancements, assigned duties, shifts, or any other condition of employment or career development."[12]

Du Pont is another company with a highly regarded program for dealing with sexual harassment. It provides a telephone hot line through which employees may report incidents and discuss options for actions without having to reveal their identity. Du Pont staff members are also encouraged to report instances of sexual harassment to their supervisors, who are obligated to take immediate action. If the accusations warrant an investigation, both the accused individual and the other staff members will be interviewed. Since the company initiated its policy in 1988 it has handled significantly more sexual harassment complaints internally and fewer in court.

While Corning, Inc., AT&T, and Du Pont serve as examples of what companies should be doing, unfortunately many businesses have not followed their lead. Some small concerns claim that they don't have the time or money with which to implement the necessary staff training regimes. In other instances, company policies on sexual harassment lack specifics as to precisely what behavior is offensive or what remedies are available. Still other companies may either fail to vigorously enforce their own rules or only educate and train their upper management rather than the entire work force. An Oakland, California, business consultant on sexual harassment described how the problem is frequently handled: "It's the unique company that takes it seriously enough to spend time and money to train their [entire] work force to let them know about the policy, instead of just tacking it to a bulletin board."[13]

Market conditions and the economy also have a bearing on how much attention and funding are devoted to handling sexual harassment cases. Many businesses struggling to survive an economic recession, such as that of the early 1990s, may be less likely to develop a firm commitment to addressing and stamping out sexual harassment than they would be in better economic times. Dr. Baila Zeitz, who helped write a book evaluating corporate reactions to sexual harassment, noted that "Corporations are more concerned about putting out fires now [just staying afloat] because of the changes that have occurred since my research. . . . They're not concerned with the niceties as much."[14]

Besides contending with financial difficulties, some companies have expressed the view that no degree of training or corporate intervention can bring about the cultural changes necessary to stem the subtler forms of sexual harassment such as viewing women differently or responding to them in an inappropriate tone. These corporations believe that changes of this nature have to come from within. One New York educator described this way of thinking: "Unless a man is planning to run for political office, [be nominated for the] Supreme Court, or some other high position, [these changes] are not going to alter his behavior. Change will happen [only when] women insist that they be treated with dignity and respect."[15]

Perhaps as roles and expectations between the sexes change over the years, stringent laws against sexual harassment will be less essential as, hopefully, behavioral standards will have been permanently raised. As long as some sectors of our society remain indifferent to this important issue, however, sexually harassed women will be forced to seek redress in court, often at a high cost to both themselves and industry.

4
Sexual Harassment in Schools

When discussing sexual harassment, people usually picture it occurring in the workplace. Yet educational environments have also long been ripe breeding grounds for this behavior. In 1986, as a sophomore at North Gwinnett High School in suburban Atlanta, Christine Franklin claimed to have experienced it firsthand when her economics teacher began making inappropriate sexual advances to her.

Their relationship had begun innocently enough. The previous year the teacher had befriended the teen, often allowing her to help him grade tests and papers. But as the months passed, his feelings for the young girl grew more intense and their interaction became somewhat unsavory. He'd frequently call Christine out of class for one thing or another, and even phoned her at home. Franklin further alleged that after a time the teacher began questioning her about affectionate behavior between herself and her boyfriend. During these discussions, which took place when they were alone in his office, the teacher shared details about intimacies he'd experienced with his wife as well as asking Christine if she'd ever considered "doing it" with an older man.

In court documents, Christine Franklin contended that the sexual harassment continued for fifteen months. During this period, the teacher pressured the young teen into having sex with him several times on the school's premises.

Franklin later revealed what had taken place when she

learned that a second young woman might be in jeopardy. As she stated, "Another student came up to me during school one day and said, 'Well, I hear these rumors about you and this [teacher].' And I just said, you know, 'I don't know what you're talking about.' And then she said, 'Well, he's been asking me questions and he's been saying things to me.' And when I thought about it, that's exactly what he said to me the year before and I felt that this was going to happen all over again, but to someone else."[1]

Knowing that she had to do something to end this sexual exploitation, Franklin reported the abuse to both a teacher and a school counselor. The counselor took the matter to the principal, who called Franklin's mother to inform her that her daughter was making up stories about a faculty member. When Christine came home that afternoon her mother confronted her with the principal's accusations and asked, "Why are you doing this?" After Christine explained what she'd been through, however, her family believed and supported her.

It wasn't easy for Franklin to return to school after that, but she knew that she had to go on with her life. School officials did not vigorously investigate her sexual harassment charges; at one point the band director even urged her to drop the matter to avoid public embarrassment. Franklin, however, was not about to back down. She filed a complaint with the Office of Civil Rights, and following an investigation it was determined that her rights had indeed been violated under Title IX of the Civil Rights Act. The sexual harassment Franklin experienced was believed to have interfered with her ability to receive an equal opportunity education.

Christine Franklin's attorney, Michael Weinstock, then initiated a civil action in the federal district court in Atlanta. However, the judge threw the case out of court on the grounds that Franklin was a student rather than an employee and was therefore not eligible to sue for damages. When her attorney took her case to Georgia's appeals court, it upheld the district court's original decision. But Franklin's case eventually reached the U.S. Supreme Court, which unanimously determined that she had the right to sue. Feminist groups throughout the country were pleased with the nine-to-nothing decision, which also happened to be the first sexual harassment case in which Clarence Thomas participated.

Although students now have legal options when faced with sexual harassment, many doubt that such reprisals will be sufficient to halt this often insidious practice. Fifteen-year-old Katy Lyle, who attended Central High in Duluth, Minnesota, also endured a high degree of sexual harassment over an eighteen-month period. Although at the time Lyle hadn't even begun dating, explicit sexual remarks were written about her in the school's boys' bathroom. Katy had to attend school while some of the students chuckled over such embarrassing descriptive slogans as "Katie Lyle blanks dogs," "Katie Lyle is a whore," and "Katie Lyle is a sex slave." Although the fifteen-year-old noted that the unsophisticated graffiti authors had even misspelled her name, it was still extremely difficult to handle what was happening.

"It got carried into the classroom and the hallways," she explained. "People would yell things at me across the hall [such as] 'I went to the bathroom in your stall this morning, Katy,' and things like that. So it affected my school life. I went home and cried every day and I hated school."[2]

To worsen the situation, many of the people with whom Lyle interacted on a daily basis were unsympathetic to her plight. Her girlfriends told her that she had blown the situation out of proportion and that she should instead try to make light of it. One male guidance counselor who attempted to help Lyle proved unable to have the writing removed from the lavatory stall.

When Lyle complained to the school authorities she was told, "We'll take care of it," but after two months the graffiti was still there. At that point Katy's mother went to school to insist that the obscene remarks be removed. But those in charge just tried to placate her, saying things like, "This is a high school," "It'll make Katy a stronger girl," and "This won't affect her. People don't read it." Although Katy and her family complained to the school sixteen times, the writing stayed on the bathroom stall for a year and a half. Disillusioned by the lack of outside intervention, Katy's brother finally removed the offensive scribbles with a cleaning solution. It took him less than a minute to complete a task that school authorities had delayed all those months.

When the administration wasn't helpful in resolving the problem, Katy Lyle contacted a women's organization in her city. Through it she learned that sexual harassment can be as devastating as physical assault. "It totally diminished my self-esteem and it robbed two years of my life and I've been trying hard to get that back," Lyle revealed. "[At first] I didn't connect that this harassment was hurting me. I didn't even know it was really harassment. Lots of people don't realize that harassment can hurt. And once I realized that harassment was what was making me feel so bad, I started to feel better instantly and realized that I was wrong. And I blamed myself for a long time and I realized that it wasn't my fault that this happened to me."[3]

Lyle decided to sue her high school in court for its lackadaisical attitude in ironing out her dilemma. Fortunately Minnesota, Lyle's home state, was one of the few states that already had a law specifically prohibiting sexual harassment in schools. An amendment to an antidiscrimination statute in Minnesota recognizes sexual harassment as "unwelcome sexual advances" or "physical contact or communication of a sexual nature" when it constitutes "an intimidating, hostile, or offensive environment" either in the workplace or within an educational environment.

Since the incident occurred prior to the Supreme Court's decision permitting students to sue schools for damages for sexual harassment, Lyle sued under the Minnesota statute. After her attorney had filed charges with the state and prepared for a trial, the Board of Education and Lyle's family agreed on an out-of-court settlement clarifying the school's sexual harassment policy as well as affording the young woman $15,000 for what she'd been through.

Although it frequently goes unrecognized or ignored, countless young people are sexually harassed in high school and even junior high. The process has been compared to a kind of terrorism, which may be randomly targeted at any student. Often the harassers in these situations are adults in positions of authority, who can influence the individual's grade or her recommendation for a summer institute or scholarship.

At times, however, sexual harassment from teenage peers can be comparably devastating. At one California high school a girl who'd been tormented by suggestive remarks from boys in her computer course was forced to transfer out of the class. "I couldn't believe that they were saying those things to my face," she complained. "The teacher had no control at all. And the other girls were too scared to stick up for me. They thought it would happen to them." Both male and female high school students agree that sexual harassment frequently escalates when boys get together in groups. "Then everybody's competing for attention," one junior high school male observed. "And one way to get it is to do something obscene."[4]

One girl, who'd been harassed by several boys almost since she entered high school, found the situation particularly difficult to deal with. On at least three separate occasions, boys had touched her body and shouted obscenities at her. Once it happened in the cafeteria lunch line and another time during class. Before long there wasn't anywhere at school where she didn't feel vulnerable.

She spoke to both her counselor and her father about what was happening. Yet when her father saw the principal he was told, "It's an isolated incident and you're blowing it way out of proportion." A later discussion with the girl's counselor revealed similar sentiments when he added, "Well, there's twenty-five hundred students in this school. What do you expect us to do?"[5]

Although sufficient evidence had accumulated to press criminal charges against the guilty boys, the girl's father declined to do so after the principal was unable to assure him that there'd be no reprisals against his daughter by others at school. The situation was finally resolved with the girl being taken out of school and taught by her parents at home. She'd found a way to avoid the harassment, but at a great personal cost.

The girl's boyfriend, upset about what had happened to her as well as to other girls at school, wanted desperately to change the situation. He, along with another girl, designed and circulated flyers protesting the continuing sexual harassment of students. After being encouraged by a teacher to work with the school on the issue, he and a small committee of similarly minded students met with the administration a number of times.

However, the teens soon realized that school officials were less interested in preventing harassment than in quelling the students' protest. These young people wanted annual mandatory seminars on sexual harassment to provide offenders with information on the legal consequences of this behavior, as well as to offer harassed young women counseling resources. Yet whenever they brought up their goals they were told, "Don't—[just] take what you can get. Don't push for any more." A seminar on the topic was eventually given, but as attendance wasn't made a school requirement, the concerned students seriously doubted whether any offenders would come. They were also disappointed in the administration for relying on the students to publicize the seminar themselves, not even including it in the daily listing of school events when it was finally scheduled.

Some good did result from the students' efforts; the school later developed a written policy on sexual harassment containing a number of the students' recommendations. Yet the small group was disappointed again; the policy wasn't automatically issued to the entire student body. According to one of the students involved, "I got sick of talking to a brick wall and I went on and I showed up at a school board meeting and gave a speech in front of the superintendent and we still got—we got nowhere until the policy came out—and even now that's the only place the policy has come out at the beginning of the second semester on a 'Take it if you want it' basis. None of these guys are getting hit. They're not hitting the problem head-on."[6]

Nevertheless, written policies that define and clarify sexual harassment may be becoming somewhat more commonplace in some of the nation's high schools. In fact, Amherst [Massachusetts] Regional High School's sexual harassment policy, which was included in the student handbook distributed in the fall of 1990, generated a good deal of attention from both educators and the general public. The policy was regarded as particularly important because it lists precisely those behaviors that the school considers harassment. These include staring or leering with sexual overtones; spreading sexual gossip; unwanted sexual comments; pressure for sexual activity; and unwanted physical contact of a sexual nature. The possible consequences cited for offenders are parent conference; apology to the victim; suspension; recommendation for expulsion from school; and referral to police. The policy also indicates that reprisals, threats, or intimidation of the sexually harassed individual will be treated as serious offenses, which could result in expulsion.

The policy encourages sexually harassed students or those with questions about the issue to seek assistance from a trusted adult such as a teacher, guidance counselor, parent or guardian, dean of students, or administrator. The school further ensures that a high degree of confidentiality will be maintained to protect both the harassed individual and the accused offender. Special efforts are also made to preserve the harassed person's sense of control over the situation.

Feminists who applaud the creation of high school sexual harassment policies stress the need for additional ways to curb the problem, to reduce the number of emotionally and financially draining lawsuits. Some want channels set up in every school through which these incidents can be discussed and promptly resolved.

At times some schools have employed a technique that involves writing a letter to the harasser. Initially developed in the 1980s in the *Harvard Business Review,* this method of handling sexual harassment was later adapted for high school students by a New England educational specialist. Using this technique, the harassed person writes a letter to the offender stating precisely what she perceives as the problem, how his behavior makes her feel, and her options if he refuses to stop. Often the correspondence is composed with the assistance of a parent or guidance counselor.

These letters frequently prove to be productive and therapeutic for the harassed person, as they provide a quiet form of immediate intervention. Although there aren't available statistics on their effectiveness in high school settings, the letters have a 90-percent success rate in employment situations. Frequently the harassment stops at once. Also often beneficial to sexually harassed students are the peer helper programs already established in many schools, in which the harassed person can reveal her predicament in a supportive atmosphere.

These remedies and others are becoming increasingly important as American educators realize that sexually harassed students are beginning to reject the old "boys will be boys" status quo. The new seriousness with which many junior high and high school administrators are beginning to view harassment cases was reflected by a junior high school assistant principal, who noted that the recent publicized cases had persuaded him "to take a harder look at what I do," especially regarding sexual harassment complaints. "I hope we will all be more in tune with where these kids are coming from," he added. "We can't side-step this issue anymore by saying 'Honey, he didn't mean it.'"[8]

Although sexual harassment undeniably exists in junior

high and high schools, it's reported to be rampant on college campuses throughout the country. Sexual harassment of college students is not a new phenomenon, especially when it occurs between professors and their students; there may be some truth to the old saying, "Where there has been a student body, there has always been a faculty for love." Ever since women were admitted to college in the 1800s, numerous female students have been pressured into having sex with their instructors.

Some college and university campus committees have done surveys to determine just how widespread the problem is. One such study conducted in 1979–80 by the University of Rhode Island indicated that female students were sexually harassed by their teachers in 53 percent of the reported cases, while the professors' graduate assistants were the culprits 8 percent of the time. Grades or exams were cited as intimidation factors in 58 percent of the incidents.

An American Council on Education publication assessing the predicament describes how college women are sexually harassed. "Verbally, a professor [may say] 'Your sweater looks big enough for both of us.' Or he may invade the woman's personal space, by touching a pin on her blouse while commenting on its ostensible beauty. . . . Or he may, as in one case reported, make sexual overtures, which, when rebuffed, led him to fail the woman student. . . . The same man was later overheard telling a colleague that he did not bother to read her exam. Unfortunately, this kind of overt unprofessionalism is infrequently reported."[9]

For years the majority of sexually harassed college students either silently endured the abuse or tried to handle the situation without involving the school administration or courts. Their reasons for doing so sometimes included an irrational fear that they were responsible for the episode or that by calling attention to a sexual incident they'd focus the faculty's attention on their gender rather than on their academic ability. Some expressed concern that their complaint would not be believed or taken seriously, while still others voiced the fear of reprisals by the offender or his colleagues.

Aware of their powerlessness against respected faculty members, female students sometimes think that to survive scholastically they have to acquiesce to the offender's demands. While high school teachers may be able to affect a student's grade, college recommendation, or scholarship chances, in some instances college professors can dramatically influence their students' career prospects or admission to highly selective graduate programs. At times a professor may even directly imply that he can help the student's career when he propositions her. As one student related her experience, "I see male colleagues and professors chumming it up and hear all this talk about making the old boy network operate for women, so I thought nothing of accepting an invitation from a professor to attend a gathering at his house. Other . . . students were present. Should I have stayed home? Was I asking for what I got? I say no. Anyway, the professor made a fool of himself pursuing me (it took me a while to catch on) and then blurted out, 'You know I want to sleep with you. You know I can do a lot for you, I have a great deal of influence. Now, of course I don't want to force you into anything, but I'm sure you're going to be sensible about this.' "[10]

College professors who've engaged in sexual relations with their students frequently argue that the young women in question were over eighteen years of age and consenting adults. However, in professor/student relationships, the issue of consent is not always as clear-cut as it might seem. A student can never be the professor's equal in a romantic relationship due to the tremendous inequities in power between the two. Even if the student isn't fully conscious of it, she may not act as freely or openly as she would with a male peer. Often the student may not even realize that she was more attracted to the status and glamour of being with a professor than she was to the actual individual.

Many professors who habitually date students have an

extensive history of seducing these often naive young women and view each term's new assortment of coeds as a human buffet of sorts. However, the student a professor is currently interested in may have no idea of his past, and may instead believe that she's special, perhaps even the woman he intends to marry. When she realizes that she's only one in a long line of previously seduced students, she may feel angry, humiliated, and abused. One young woman recounted her seduction by her archaeology professor:

> I guess that I fell for my Lebanese archaeology professor Dr. Hakim [not his real name] my first week at school. I remember thinking that he was a combination of Einstein-level genius and movie-star material. He was tall, dark, and handsome, with the kind of charm that sweeps you off your feet.
>
> You can't imagine how thrilled I was when he picked me to be his student assistant on the work-study program. It was great to be around him, he knew everything about archaeology and was well respected in his field. Being with him broadened my mind, but it was more than that. Dr. Hakim made me feel pretty. He'd stroke my long light brown hair and say that in his country men go wild for women with golden tresses. Whenever I wore a miniskirt he'd say that I had great legs. I never felt as wonderful as when I was with him. But as it turned out that feeling didn't last for very long.
>
> I'd dreamt of dating him, marrying him, and of making world-renowned archaeological discoveries with him. But at first these were just an eighteen-year-old's fantasies. We were only friends until the last day of the term, when while I was typing in his office Dr. Hakim suddenly grabbed and kissed me.
>
> Then he said, "Ann [not her real name], I don't want the end of the term to be the end of us. I want to see you at least once a week and maybe more often if we can find the time." He asked me if we could get together that Thursday without meeting at his office for once. I agreed and asked

if we'd be going to a museum or taking in a movie. I'd already begun thinking how great it would be to view ancient artifacts with such a brilliant archaeologist. But apparently Dr. Hakim had no intention of looking at mideastern art objects with me. Instead he simply smiled and said, "Why Ann, I thought that we'd go to a motel."

At that moment my heart fell straight to the pit of my stomach. I had a crush on Dr. Hakim and had liked it when he kissed me, but somehow I never imagined going to a motel with him. As ridiculous as it may sound now, I'd only fantasized about our being married—you know, a white wedding gown, peach-colored flowers, my parents and friends at the chapel—the whole bit. Maybe Dr. Hakim hadn't realized that I was an eighteen-year-old virgin. Or worse yet, maybe he didn't care.

But that didn't matter back then. I was in love for the first time in my life and I trusted my archaeology professor. Even if he didn't propose immediately, I thought that we'd be married before long in any case.

We never went to a museum, or out to dinner, or even to a movie. In fact we never went anywhere except to his apartment. We had sex on our first date, if you can call just going to bed a date, and we continued to "date" that way for the next nineteen months. I'd have done anything to please Dr. Hakim, but I always felt ashamed of our relationship. I think that's because he carefully kept me hidden away from everyone that mattered in his life. When he was around other faculty members, he barely acknowledged me. I'd watch my friends go to fraternity parties and football games with boys from school, while I stayed at the dorm waiting for his calls to tell me when to come to his apartment.

Yet I still felt that I loved him and whenever he wanted sex he'd tell me that he loved me too. I'd been brought up to believe that when two people fell in love they'd spend the rest of their lives together. But when I finally worked up enough nerve to approach the topic, I realized for the first time that Dr. Hakim had never had any intention of marrying me. By then I just felt overwhelmed with hurt and shame.

A few months later Dr. Hakim stopped calling me. He said that if I was always going to be so petulant when we were together, there was no point in our continuing to see one another. I heard that he began seeing another student within weeks and I later found out that he'd even dated other girls while we were together. It didn't feel good to learn that you were just one on a long list of "consenting adults."

I hated him for taking advantage of me and I hated myself for not having realized what was happening sooner. But I'd never been a match for him. Dr. Hakim had been all over the world on various archaeological assignments, while I'd never been out of Connecticut. He was a smooth talker too; now I realize that all the appealing things he told me over the months had probably been tried out on other girls before me.

It was as if he stole nearly twenty months of my life and love. Months during which I should have been going out with my friends and boys my own age. They say that all is fair in love and war, but what happened to me wasn't fair. I still feel dirty every time I think about the professor I once revered.

Studies show that education in America has traditionally served to largely reinforce "women's dependency and reliance on authority." Some research findings underscore the fact that "women are taught submission, not aggression." It's also been demonstrated that "They learn that being 'good' implies not acting but reacting, not trusting oneself but entrusting oneself to the authorities—parents, clergy, teachers—who promise reward. Forced into a choice between a teacher's wishes and their own, some students do what they have learned to do best—defer, submit, agree. In their own peculiar ways, they once again act out the roles of 'good little girls,' doing what teacher says is best."[11]

The question of what constitutes genuine "consent" and

the inherent exploitation in teacher/student sexual relationships was addressed by the American Association of University Professors in 1983, when the group proposed guidelines on sexual harassment to its national membership. The standard of teacher/student behavior described below is now considered an integral part of professional conduct on campus:

> Intimate relationships between professors and students are regarded with suspicion because they pose conflicts with faculty responsibilities and ethics. The prevailing view among academicians is that the faculty member's job is to teach students. Whenever he chooses to treat his women students differently from the men, to become more than a professor, he manipulates his role and endangers his professionalism. Men professors [generally] do not kiss, fondle, or comment on the appearances of male students, and most maintain that there is no reason to treat women differently.[12]

Unfortunately, the problem of sexual harassment on campus is not limited to faculty exploitation of students. Many college women have also been harassed by male students. Frequently college women may be forced to endure the same type of harassment high school females encounter, although at times the problem is even more intense. To help stop the harassment, some college women's groups have devised precise guidelines to define sexual harassment. Like the sexually harassed high school students, these women believe that it is necessary to pinpoint the offensive behaviors in order to curb them.

In its assessment of sexual harassment, the Columbia-Barnard Task Force against Sexual Coercion includes "offensive" remarks that "evoke sexual stereotypes or generalizations," while the Association of American Colleges' Project on the Status of Education of Women goes even further. Under the term "peer harassment," the group lists efforts to make females a "negative reference group, male domination of class discussions, and a practice known as the elephant walk." The elephant walk consists of a male exposing his penis and pulling out his pants pockets to imitate an elephant's trunk and ears.

Unfortunately, like their high school counterparts, sexually harassed college students also initially found that a large number of school administrations hesitated to act on their complaints. This might have been partly due to the fear that the adverse publicity generated by these incidents might further diminish the already declining enrollment at some institutions. Even in instances in which colleges dealt with harassment cases, the injured parties frequently felt that the penalties were inappropriately light.

That's what happened one spring when a high school senior visited an exclusive Ivy League school in the East prior to her enrollment the following fall. While at a college fraternity party that weekend, she met a boy who asked her to walk him back to his dorm. As it was a pleasantly warm April evening and the boy had seemed interesting to talk to, she agreed. But after they arrived and she turned to walk back, he pulled her toward him to kiss her. When she struggled to free herself from his grasp, the young man kissed her hard on the neck. Then he finally released her, saying, "It's okay, you can go. I've left my mark on you."

The girl was outraged, but as there was little she could do to rectify matters, she tried to put it out of her mind. But that was easier said than done. Even a year and a half after enrolling at the university, the feelings of powerlessness and humiliation she experienced that night resurfaced whenever she saw the boy on campus.

The situation worsened once she learned that the same student had rough-handled another girl, as well as attained the prestigious position of editor-in-chief of the college review. "I had extreme loathing for this person," she explained. "His being in a position of authority showed how completely he'd gotten away with his assaults. His life was hunky-dory, while I had to live with the attack every day."

Unable to push down her feelings any longer, the young woman filed charges against the offender. To her dismay, however, school officials did not take her case very seriously. Instead of referring the incident to the Committee on Standards, which was empowered to recommend either suspension or expulsion from the university, it was only scheduled for a dean's hearing. The punishments ensuing from a dean's hearing are significantly lighter—frequently the guilty person may only be required to apologize to the offended individual. The sexually harassed young woman became so discouraged by the school's response that she made plans to transfer to another college.

Since the administration had taken her case so lightly, the harassed woman's friends decided to alert the women on campus to the harasser's presence. They put up posters with his picture on it and the warning "Beware of This Man" and "How Many More Women Will Be Hurt?" Their desperate response was not unusual. In the fall of 1990 women at Brown University similarly took matters into their own hands due to their school administration's lax attitude toward sexual harassment on campus. The Brown students began posting a list of male harassers in the women's lavatory.

At still another school, women from the two college sororities joined together to draft letters to school officials to protest the unfair and abusive treatment of college women. They stated, "Amid recent rumors of alleged acts involving voyeurism, sexual harassment, and sexual assault, we feel the need to express our outrage. We have been silent too long. Witnesses to these crimes who have not come forward are equally responsible. . . . By breaking our silence and acknowledging the problem, we are ending our inadvertent acceptance of these atrocities." While the "atrocities" referred to in the letter may have been previously regarded as little more than the typical distasteful pranks characteristic of male college youths, it was becoming increasingly clear that a new wave of sensitivity to sexual harassment was sweeping many of our nation's centers of learning.

As in some American high schools, the growing awareness of and refusal to accept sexual harassment at institutions of higher learning has prompted changes in many college and university administration policies. In the past few years, a number of colleges have hired permanent full-time sexual harassment counselors. These counselors help both male and female students to see common campus injustices as part of a larger, more pervasive social problem. Frequently these counselors sponsor campus seminars and workshops on the power differences between men and women. In addition to consciousness-raising and clarifying dating expectations, the counselors also serve as advocates for sexually harassed students who may be reluctant to come forward to largely male administrations.

Some colleges and universities are also instituting broad-based changes to deal with those students and professors who harass. These include

• Instituting clearly written policies on sexual harassment and the penalties for it.

• Sponsoring a designated number of workshops and lectures throughout the school term to publicize the issue. Sexual harassment counselors stress that this abuse cannot be halted by policies known only to the college committee members who wrote them. They feel that the majority of harassers would stop if they were made aware of their actions' consequences.

• Establishing grievance procedures for sexually harassed individuals. This measure enables students to know precisely whom to see about the problem and the various steps involved in filing a formal complaint.

• Instituting special committees to investigate charges and seek a fair resolution.

• Providing informal mediation to allow the offender an opportunity to correct his behavior prior to initiating formal disciplinary measures.

- Keeping any campus centers or offices established to assist sexually harassed students well informed, properly staffed, and sufficiently funded to carry out the duties assigned them.

As might be expected, sexual harassment in education does not stop at college-level institutions. Through the years there have been frequent incidents of it in postgraduate programs and various professional schools. Among those cases that have made headlines is that of Dr. Frances Conley, one of the nation's first female neurosurgeons.

Despite her outstanding ability, Conley, a professor at Stanford University School of Medicine, had endured countless episodes of sexual harassment both while training as a neurosurgeon and as a medical school faculty member. During the time she studied neurosurgery, Dr. Conley felt she was not taken seriously by many of her professors, who doubted that a woman could ever be firmly committed to such a grueling career. Besides often being treated as an ornament, the young female physician was also subjected to inappropriate touching, sexual propositions, and sexist teasing and jokes.

Yet despite her humiliation at being treated that way, Conley never complained or revealed her true feelings. To do so would have made her an outcast and perhaps even ruined her chances of becoming a neurosurgeon. So instead she learned to play by their humiliating rules while managing to quietly evade some of her especially lascivious teachers and colleagues.

Later on, as a respected neurosurgeon and medical school professor, Conley still found herself continually subjected to sexist remarks and gestures. The situation grew even worse once a different chairman took over her department at the medical school. The new department head was extremely chauvinistic and before long excluded Conley from important departmental decisions and duties. When she protested his treatment of her, she'd be characterized as either "difficult" to work with or suffering from PMS.

Rather than continue to tolerate this abuse, Frances Conley resigned from her position. At first, she'd intended to leave quietly, but after chairing a series of school seminars which dealt somewhat with sexual harassment, Conley realized that her experiences were not unique. Other female medical students and doctors were being treated as she'd been and little had actually changed since 1968, when Conley first began her neurosurgical training. One woman at the forum told how an older male physician had fondled her breasts, while others present revealed that caricatures of naked females were sometimes used to liven up medical school lectures.

Dr. Frances Conley's subsequent decision to publicly acknowledge the reasons for her resignation initiated a nationwide discussion about sexual harassment in education. Her outspokenness in calling attention to this problem also caused Stanford, along with other medical schools, to reexamine its administrative policies. At the insistence of many of her colleagues, Conley rejoined the medical school's staff the following year to work for change from within.

5
What You Can Do

Despite recent legal strides and gains in public awareness, the problem of sexual harassment still exists. Although women may continue to be harassed in school and work settings, that doesn't mean that they have to put up with it. In these instances, it is especially important for the woman not to blame herself. As a spokesperson for the National Association for the Professional Saleswoman expressed it, "Damage occurs when the woman takes responsibility for the incident. 'What did I do wrong to make this person do this,' may be her reaction, when the problem is his, not hers. . . . If all women put the responsibility where it belongs rather than adjusting their own behavior, these offenders might [still] not get the message, but the women would be happier and more productive."[1]

Many sexual harassment counselors advise taking the following steps to resolve these situations:

• Keep an ongoing record of the harasser's offensive behavior. Write a brief description of what occurred, including the date, time, and circumstances surrounding the incident. Note the names of any witnesses to the interaction and be sure to make copies of these records as you gather them.

• Find out if your school or company has a mechanism in place to handle sexual harassment complaints, and if the problem persists, use it. If such channels aren't available, remind your company's personnel office that employers and educational institutions are legally responsible for maintaining a harassment-free environment. Students should have a parent or guardian speak to school authorities.

• If you are dissatisfied with your company's response, contact the nearest field office of the Equal Employment Opportunity Commission (EEOC). A representative there can provide support and further information regarding alternatives. A list of these offices is provided at the back of this book. If the harassment continues in a school setting, consider exploring your alternatives with an attorney who specializes in this area of the law. However, make certain you are aware of any fees involved beforehand, since these costs can mount up quickly.

If you pursue legal channels in resolving a sexual harassment case, it is extremely important to be able to back up your accusations. Between 1981 and 1992 the number of formal sexual harassment complaints annually filed more than doubled, but unfortunately the majority of these women lost in court. Attorneys report that plaintiffs without clear-cut cases of sexual harassment are often wasting their time.

These sentiments were recently borne out by a study conducted by professors David Tempstra, of the University of Idaho, and Douglas Baker, of Washington State University. These researchers reviewed the harassment charges filed with the Illinois Department of Human Resources over a two-year period. Only 31 percent of the women who sued during that time won their cases. Those who fared best in court had leveled such serious charges as sexual assault, unwarranted physical contact, or direct threats of job loss for denied sexual favors. Women charging milder forms of sexual harassment, including being exposed to offensive language, whistles, or undesired requests for dates, were considerably less likely to do well in the judicial system.

However, those who built up their cases by identifying and bringing in witnesses as well as formally notifying their employers of their intent to sue enhanced their chances for success. "If they had just one of three factors in their favor—witnesses, serious charges, [or] management notice—their chances [of winning] were significantly greater than 31 percent," Professor Tempstra stated. "With all three factors, they had a definite chance of winning their case." Such successful plaintiffs often received well-deserved promotions, the right to a job change within their corporation, or a cash award. The researchers concluded that "Individuals considering filing formal sexual harassment charges should carefully consider the relative strengths and weaknesses of their case."[2] They suggest that, prior to initiating court action, potential plaintiffs amass and carefully review all relevant documents to best evaluate their chances in a legal showdown.

Yet not everyone who is sexually harassed feels able or prepared to handle the problem through the courts. Women in school or work environments that have sexual harassment policies may feel most comfortable using those channels. But a sexually harassed person at a school or company lacking both a written policy and a sympathetic administration or management team may find the following counselor-recommended practices helpful. Anyone who attempts these tactics, however, must remember that there is no guaranteed way to end harassment without outside intervention. Some offenders continue the abuse regardless of what the woman does and are only stopped through suspension or expulsion from school, job loss, or court action. Nevertheless, in other situations, these measures have proven extremely helpful.

- *Use Direct Confrontation*

Directly confronting the offender sometimes works, since the harasser knows that if his objectionable behavior comes to the attention of school officials or his employer his future could be seriously affected. In speaking to the offender, the woman should not smile or act coyly out of embarrassment, as this could confuse the important message being delivered.

Counselors suggest that the woman simply tell the man that his behavior will no longer be tolerated.

In one such instance, a male coworker had put his arm around a woman's waist at the company water cooler and tightly squeezed her. She immediately removed his hand, looked him squarely in the face, and said, "Don't ever do that to me again." She was delighted to find that he never did.

- **Use Humorous Reminders of Possible Repercussions**

    Women harassed by their married supervisors or professors have sometimes found a subtle reminder of possible unpleasant repercussions more effective than direct confrontation. There are no hard-and-fast rules in these situations; each woman must gauge what she feels the offender will be most responsive to.

    A secretary who resented being asked to accompany her boss on a business trip and share his room responded, "Well, I guess this is just your way of asking me to marry you. I never realized that you were so shy or that you cared for me that way. But before we can go away together, you'll have to get a divorce. Do you want to talk to your wife with me there or should I call her myself? Sometimes these things are easier to hear coming from a woman."

    The startled supervisor looked at her as though she were out of her mind, but he nevertheless dropped the issue. The secretary was obviously too valuable an employee to lose, yet he must have felt that a personal involvement with her was far too risky for a married man.

- **Leave the Scene**

    Depending on the situation and the nature of the harassment, it may be safest to avoid any form of confrontation with the harasser. This may be especially true for women who find themselves alone in an isolated area with the harasser after a school or social event, or working late by themselves at an office with a client or salesperson they don't know well. In such predicaments being direct or creative with the offender may be less desirable than quickly heading for the nearest exit.

When a clothing-store buyer who agreed to stay late to see a salesman whose plane had been delayed had the misfortune of having him caress her breast as he brushed past her, she packed up her belongings and left the premises. He called the following day to apologize, but she refused to deal with him a second time and instead referred him to a male colleague.

• *Avoid Alcoholic Beverages at Business Functions (for individuals of legal drinking age)*

Choosing not to drink following dinner meetings is a good way of emphasizing your professionalism and stressing that you are there for business rather than social reasons. "I've stopped drinking since I've been in this business," one exceptionally successful saleswoman noted. "You can lose control of a situation if you drink or be perceived by others as losing it.... If I know a client has a tendency to drink too much, I just don't have lunch or dinner with him."

• *Become One of the Boys*

A good way for women to shield themselves from potential sexual harassment in work situations is to make certain that their male colleagues view them as part of the team. At times this may involve some extra effort on their part, but most working women believe the potential rewards are worth it.

One woman, whose company did not have a central office in the New York suburb where she lived, worked out of her home about three days a week. However, on Friday evenings, all the salesmen would meet at a city restaurant to discuss their accounts and new business leads. Although it wasn't always convenient for her to do so, the woman made a point of coming into the city each week to join them. She exchanged news and valuable ideas with the others and was seen as an important member of the sales force rather than a sex object or challenge.

Some women report that extending professional courtesies to male coworkers also deters sexual harassment. One successful businesswoman offered the following tip as an example of what can be done: "If you're requesting tickets to take a customer to a ball game, order a few extra and invite some of your colleagues. They'll appreciate the gesture and know that you're willing to share." A woman who is not in a position to invite clients and coworkers out for the day can scale down the gesture to correspond with her position in the firm.

- *Don't Offer a Shoulder to Cry On*

In our culture women are frequently taught to be more sympathetic than men to other people's problems. Unfortunately, some men who sexually harass women use this to their advantage. These offenders exploit the female's compassion to personalize their work relationship. They want the woman to feel sorry for them so that she'll be especially vulnerable to their sexual advances.

While it is advisable for a woman to have a cordial relationship with her male coworkers and supervisors, it is not necessary to act as their therapist or ever to be subjected to hearing the intimate details of their sex lives.

- *Avoid Being Inappropriately Friendly*

Some women find it helpful to maintain professional boundaries in their work relationships with men. They believe that it's best not to become any more involved than is necessary to pleasantly and adequately meet their job requirements. One woman who felt that a male colleague had been lasciviously staring at her legs simply refused when he asked her to go for a bite to eat after work. She merely said, "Thank you, but I never mix business with pleasure." She knew that she had made her point shortly thereafter, when his prolonged gazes and invitations out abruptly stopped. In situations where it's awkward not to socially mix with male coworkers and supervisors, it's a good idea to suggest that both people's spouses or dates come along.

- ***Seek Out Female Networking Opportunities***

    Women's networking groups in various professions are springing up in many parts of the country. Networking involves meeting and sharing professional opportunities, thoughts, feelings, and ideas with similarly employed women. At some colleges and universities, comparable support services may be available on campus. Such experiences can be extremely beneficial in learning successful ways to cope with a broad range of often troublesome predicaments, including sexual harassment.

- ***Pay Attention to Your Instincts***

    Many individuals develop a sort of sixth sense about sexual harassment. A woman who suspects that her coworker or supervisor has an unsavory interest in her may actually be picking up cues from him. It's generally advisable for women to distance themselves from men and boys who don't act within the acceptable norms of the work or school environment. Therefore, if a suspect client or coworker asks a female staff member to meet with him at six in the evening, it might be better if she suggests that they meet at nine in the morning instead. At times, discouraging an overly relaxed and informal attitude can dissuade a harasser.

    Regardless of how a woman chooses to handle the situation, it's important that she stop the harassment. Feminist organizations warn that while viewing sexually harassed females as victims generates sympathy, in the long run it could prove detrimental to women. They argue that victim status denotes a helpless individual in need of protection, while women are actually quite capable of taking control of their lives and achieving vital personal gains. As one legal expert described the problem, "The woman-as-victim is a cultural script that [does not] challenge the hierarchical structure. It's a kind of melodrama that doesn't lead to any change in the conditions that cause victimization."[3]

Today women are beginning to realize that sexual harassment need not be a fact of life. Many are banding together to exchange their victim status for new forms of empowerment. Just as women running for office have made sexual harassment a central campaign issue, labor unions as well as campus feminist groups are now petitioning businesses and educational institutions to implement even broader antiharassment policies.

Perhaps the ultimate solution lies in achieving a greater overall commitment to ending sexual harassment. Some males will have to challenge long-held beliefs and behaviors toward members of the opposite sex. Women need to continue to demand harassment-free treatment at school and work, regardless of whether they do so through court suits, legislation, or public awareness campaigns. They must be supported in this endeavor by their male friends and partners. The difficult task of halting sexual harassment still lies ahead, and it is everyone's responsibility to bring us closer to the goal.

Appendix 1
Employee Rights Legislation

At times sexual harassment cases are not clear-cut but involve other discriminatory factors. The following is a listing and brief description of the laws that safeguard employee rights.

Equal Pay Act of 1963
Requires that employees of both sexes receive equal pay for equal work

Title VII of the Civil Rights Act of 1964
Prohibits employment discrimination due to race, color, religion, sex, or national origin

Age Discrimination in Employment Act of 1967
Prohibits employers from discriminating against older workers, unless age is a necessary requirement for the job

Occupational Safety and Health Act of 1970
Requires employers to maintain a safe working environment for their staff

Vietnam Era Veterans' Readjustment Assistance Act of 1972
Requires employers awarded federal contracts of $10,000 or more to take measures to hire disabled and qualified veterans of the Vietnam War era

Vocational Rehabilitation Act of 1973
Employers awarded federal contracts of $2,500 or more must take measures to hire and promote qualified handicapped individuals

EMPLOYEE RETIREMENT INCOME SECURITY ACT OF 1974
Requires employers offering employee pension plans to maintain these plans according to federal minimum standards

PREGNANCY DISCRIMINATION ACT OF 1978
Protects pregnant women from employment discrimination

IMMIGRATION REFORM AND CONTROL ACT OF 1986
Prohibits discrimination against a job applicant on the basis of national origin, but permits employers to select a U.S. citizen over an alien if both job candidates are equally qualified

EMPLOYEE POLYGRAPH PROTECTION ACT OF 1988
Prohibits most private employers from requiring staff members or job applicants to take a polygraph test and disallows the dismissal of an employee who refuses to take such a test

WORKER ADJUSTMENT AND RETRAINING ACT OF 1988
Requires employers to provide at least sixty days' notice prior to a plant closing or massive layoffs

CIVIL RIGHTS ACT OF 1991
Reinforces and strengthens antidiscrimination provisions granted under Title VII of the Civil Rights Act of 1964

In addition to the laws listed above, several dozen federal statutes, such as the Fair Labor Standards, exist to shield workers from discrimination or dismissal for exercising their legal rights in job-related situations.

Appendix 2
Equal Employment Opportunity Offices
(listed by city)

Albuquerque, New Mexico (area office)
Suite 1105
505 Marquette, N.W., 87102
Andrew Lopez, Director
(505) 766-2061

Atlanta, Georgia (district office)
Suite 1100
75 Piedmont Avenue, N.E., 30335
Harris A. Williams, Director
(404) 331-6093

Baltimore, Maryland (district office)
Suite 4000
111 Market Place, 21202
Chris Roggerson, Director
(301) 962-3932

Birmingham, Alabama (district office)
Suite 101
1900 Third Avenue, N., 35203
Warren Boullock, Director
(205) 731-0082

Boston, Massachusetts (area office)
Room 100, 10th Floor
1 Congress Street, 02114
Charles L. Looney, Director
(617) 565-3200

Buffalo, New York (local office)
Room 301
28 Church Street, 14202
Jon Patterson, Director
(716) 846-4441

Charlotte, North Carolina (district office)
5500 Central Avenue, 28212
Curtis Todd, Acting Director
(704) 567-7100

Chicago, Illinois (district office)
Room 930-A
536 S. Clark Street, 60605
John Rowe, Director
(312) 353-2713

Cincinnati, Ohio (area office)
Room 7015
550 Main Street, 45202
Earl Haley, Director
(513) 684-2851

Cleveland, Ohio (district office)
Room 600
1375 Euclid Avenue, 44115
Harold Ferguson, Director
(216) 522-2001

Dallas, Texas (district office)
8303 Elmbrook Drive, 75247
Jacqueline Bradley, Director
(214) 767-7015

Denver, Colorado (district office)
2nd Floor
1845 Sherman Street, 80203
Francisco J. Flores, Director
(303) 866-1300

Detroit, Michigan (district office)
Room 1540
477 Michigan Avenue, 48226
A. William Schukar, Director
(313) 226-7636

El Paso, Texas (local office)
Suite 100
Building C, The Commons, 79902
Eliazar Salinas, Director
(915) 534-6558

Fresno, California (local office)
Suite 103
1313 P Street, 93721
David Rodriguez, Director
(209) 487-5793

Greensboro, North Carolina (local office)
Room 13-27
324 W. Market Street, 27402
Daisy Crenshaw, Director
(919) 333-5174

Greenville, South Carolina (local office)
Suite B41
300 E. Washington Street, 29601
Joseph M. D'Arcangelo, Director
(803) 233-1791

Honolulu, Hawaii (local office)
Suite 404
677 Ala Moana Boulevard, 96813
Linda K. Kreis, Director
(808) 541-3120

Houston, Texas (district office)
7th Floor
1919 Smith Street, 77002
Harriet J. Ehrlich, Director
(713) 653-3320

Indianapolis, Indiana (district office)
Room 456
46 E. Ohio Street, 46204
Thomas P. Hadfield, Director
(317) 226-7212

Jackson, Mississippi (area office)
207 W. Amite Street, 39269
Henrene P. Matthews, Director
(601) 965-4537

Kansas City, Missouri (area office)
10th Floor
911 Walnut, 64106
Joseph P. Doherty, Director
(816) 426-5773

Little Rock, Arkansas (area office)
Suite 621
320 W. Capital Avenue, 72201
W. P. Brown, Director
(501) 378-5060

Los Angeles, California (district office)
5th Floor
3660 Wilshire Boulevard, 90010
Dorothy Porter, Director
(213) 251-7278

Louisville, Kentucky (area office)
Room 613
601 W. Broadway, 40202
Clifford J. Johnson, Director
(502) 582-6082

Memphis, Tennessee (district office)
Suite 621
1407 Union Avenue, 38104
Walter Grabon, Director
(901) 722-2617

Miami, Florida (district office)
6th Floor
1 N.E. First Street, 33132
Fedenico Costales, Director
(305) 536-4491

Milwaukee, Wisconsin (district office)
Suite 800
310 W. Wisconsin Avenue, 53203
Chester Bailey, Director
(414) 297-1111

Minneapolis, Minnesota (local office)
Room 108
220 Second Street, S., 55401
Michael Bloyer, Director
(612) 370-3330

Nashville, Tennessee (area office)
Suite 202
50 Vantage Way, 37228
John A. Pahmeyer, Director
(615) 736-5820

Newark, New Jersey (area office)
Room 301
60 Park Place, 07102
Corrado Gigante, Director
(201) 645-6383

Appendix 3
Organizations Concerned with Sexual Harassment and Related Issues

Center for Women Policy Studies
2000 P Street, N.W., Suite 508
Washington, D.C. 20036

Center for Women's Studies and Services
2467 E Street
San Diego, California 92102

Clearinghouse on Women's Issues
P.O. Box 70603
Friendship Heights, Maryland 20813

Coal Employment Project
17 Emory Place
Knoxville, Tennessee 37917

Coalition for Women's Appointments
c/o National Women's Political Caucus
1275 K Street, N.W., Suite 750
Washington, D.C. 20005-4051

Congressional Caucus for Women's Issues
2471 Rayburn House Office Building
Washington, D.C. 20515

Federally Employed Women
1400 I Street, N.W., Suite 425
Washington, D.C. 20005

Federation of Organizations for Professional Women
2001 S Street, N.W., Suite 500
Washington, D.C. 20009

Ms. Foundation for Women
141 Fifth Avenue, Suite 6-S
New York, New York 10010

National Association of Commissions
for Women
YWCA Building M-10
624 Ninth Street, N.W.
Washington, D.C. 20001

National Black Women's Political
Leadership Caucus
3005 Bladensburg Road, N.E., No. 217
Washington, D.C. 20018

National Commission on Working Women
1325 G Street, N.W.
Washington, D.C. 20005

National Council of Career Women
1223 Potomac Street, N.W.
Washington, D.C. 20007

National Council for Research on Women
Sara Delano Roosevelt Memorial House
47–49 E. Sixty-fifth Street
New York, New York 10021

National Council of Women of the
United States
777 United Nations Plaza
New York, New York 10017

National Institute for Women of Color
1301 Twentieth Street, N.W., Suite 702
Washington, D.C. 20036

National Organization for Women
1000 Sixteenth Street, N.W., Suite 700
Washington, D.C. 20036

National Women's Party
Sewall-Belmont House
144 Constitution Avenue, N.E.
Washington, D.C. 20002

National Women's Law Center
1616 P Street
Washington, D.C. 20036

National Women's Political Caucus
1275 K Street, N.W., Suite 750
Washington, D.C. 20005

9 to 5, National Association of Working Women
614 Superior Avenue, N.W., Room 852
Cleveland Ohio, 44113

For More Information

BOOKS

Ashton-Jones, Evelyn, and Gary Olson. *The Gender Reader.* Needham Heights, Mass.: Allyn, 1991.

Conte, Alba. *Sexual Harassment in the Workplace.* New York: Wiley, 1990.

Feagin, Joe R., and Clairece B. Feagin. *Discrimination American Style: Institutional Racism and Sexism.* 2d ed. Melbourne, Fl.: Krieger, 1986.

Gregory, Jeanne. *Sex, Race and the Law: Legislating for Equality.* Newberry Park, Calif.: Sage, 1988.

Hammer, Trudy J. *Taking a Stand Against Sexism and Sex Discrimination.* New York: Franklin Watts, 1990.

Hoff, Joan. *Law, Gender and Injustice: A Legal History of U.S. Women.* New York: New York University Press, 1991.

Neville, Kathleen. *Corporate Attractions: An Inside Account of Sexual Harassment with the New Sexual Rules for Men and Women on the Job.* Reston, Va.: Acropolis Books, 1990.

Paludi, Michele. *Academic and Workplace Sexual Harassment: A Resource Manual.* Albany, N.Y.: State University of New York Press, 1991.

Quina, Kathryn, and Nancy Carlson. *Rape, Incest and Sexual Harassment: A Guide for Helping Survivors.* Westport, Conn.: Greenwood, 1989.

ARTICLES

Bruning, Fred. "Into the Den of the Dinosaur." *MacLean's* 103 (October 22, 1990): 13.

Cohen, Lloyd R. "Sexual Harassment and the Law," *Society* 28 (May–June 1991): 8.

Galen, Michelle, and Zachary Schiller. "Ending Sexual Harassment: Business Is Getting the Message." *Business Week,* March 18, 1991, 98.

Gross, Jane. "Doctor to Rejoin Stanford Staff." *New York Times* 140 (September 5, 1991): A26.

Kantrowitz, Barbara, and Heather Woodin. "Diagnosis: Harassment: A Medical School Professor Overcomes Sexual Slurs." *Newsweek* 116 (November 26, 1990): 62.

King, Peter. "Shame Has No Price." *Sports Illustrated* 73 (December 10, 1990): 86.

Leo, John. "What Qualifies as Sexual Harassment?" *U.S. News & World Report* 109 (August 13, 1990): 17.

Melville, Joy. "Acts Of Violence: Sexual Violence Against Women Is Nothing New." *New Statesman & Society* 4 (May 17, 1991): 24.

VIDEOS

At times effective sexual harassment policies and programs at schools and businesses have arisen from individual efforts. Anyone interested in organizing training seminars for students or employees might be interested in one or more of the videos listed below. These tapes may either be bought or rented.

"A Costly Proposition" (25 minutes)
This video employs five vignettes to show different aspects of sexual harassment. The film, coproduced by ABC, CBS, and NBC for their own workshops on the topic, is an extremely useful teaching tool. "Intent vs. Impact," another well-targeted video distributed by the same company, is available in two versions—one for employees and the other for management. The film demonstrates how the repercussions generated by various actions can be detrimental in a society where the rules governing the behavior of men and women are in a state of flux.

BNA Communications
9439 Key West Avenue
Rockville, Maryland 20850
(301) 948-0540

"Sexual Harassment: Walking the Corporate Fine Line"
(21 minutes)
Through a television newsmagazine format, this film documents the historical legal steps taken in the battle against sexual harassment. It emphasizes the problem's cost to both individuals and corporations, as well as providing basic information on what a corporate antiharassment policy should contain.

NOW Legal Defense and Education Fund
99 Hudson Street
New York, New York 10013
(212) 925-6635

"Sexual Harassment ... Shades of Gray" (16 to 26 minutes)
A package of five videos on sexual harassment: "What Am I Doing Here?"; "What is Sexual Harassment?"; "Cost of Sexual Harassment"; "What Does the Law Say?"; and "What Should I Do?"

In a relaxed conversational manner, these videos clearly pinpoint the most important aspects of sexual harassment. The tapes are well researched, highly informative, and easily understandable.

Pacific Resources Development Group
4044 Northeast Fifty-eighth Street
Seattle, Washington 98105
(206) 522-8671

"Sexual Harassment—A Threat to Your Profits" (20 minutes)
A video that shows how sexual harassment can have a disastrous effect on a business's staff morale, public relations, and productivity. Positive steps to prevent sexual harassment in the workplace are also provided. The video comes with a workbook that shows both the best ways to implement a company policy against sexual harassment and investigate sexual harassment complaints.

Philip Office Associates, Inc.
750 Talbot Tower
Dayton, Ohio 45402
(513) 461-1220

"Preventing Sexual Harassment in the Workplace" (60 minutes)
Featuring vignettes to illustrate the problem, this film focuses on the legal aspects of sexual harassment. A number of the video's scenarios are reenactments of actual cases.

Vencompass, Inc.
P.O. Box 6121
Brie, Pennsylvania 16512-6121
(814) 838-7490 or (800) 458-4114; (800) 352-2112 (in Pennsylvania)

Source Notes

1. SEXUAL HARASSMENT

1. ABC News "Primetime Live" #235 (March 5, 1992).
2. Ibid.
3. Ibid.
4. Ibid.
5. Barbara Kantrowitz, "Striking a Nerve," *Newsweek* 118 (October 21, 1991): 34.
6. Nancy Gibbs, "Office Crimes," *Time* 138 (October 21, 1991): 55.
7. Ibid.
8. Ibid.
9. Ted Gest and Amy Saltzman, "Harassment: Men on Trial," *U.S. News & World Report* 111 (October 21, 1991): 30.
10. Kantrowitz, "Striking A Nerve," 38.
11. Ronald Sullivan, "Penthouse Model to Fight Loss of Sex-Harassment Damages," *New York Times*, April 5, 1992, 32.
12. Ibid.

2. THOMAS/HILL: SOMEONE IS NOT TELLING THE TRUTH

1. Richard Lacayo, "A Question Of Character," *Time* 138 (October 21, 1991): 43.
2. Ibid.
3. Ibid.
4. Ibid., p. 44.
5. *Nomination of Clarence Thomas to Be an Associate Justice of the U.S. Supreme Court,* Senate Executive Report 102–15, Judoc #Y1.1/6: 102–115.
6. Ibid.
7. Ibid.
8. Jill Smolowe, "She Said, He Said," *Time* 138 (October 21, 1991): 40.

9. *Nomination of Clarence Thomas.*
10. Priscilla Painton, "Woman Power," *Time* 131 (October 28, 1991): 24.
11. *Nomination of Clarence Thomas.*
12. Eloise Salholz, "Thomas and Hill: Mentor or Tormentor?" *Newsweek* 118 (October 21, 1991): 29.
13. Painton, "Woman Power," 24.
14. Margaret Carlson, "The Ultimate Men's Club," *Time* 138 (October 21, 1991): 50.
15. Ibid.
16. Richard L. Buke, "Women Accusing Democrats of Betrayal," *New York Times*, October 17, 1991, 67.
17. Painton, "Woman Power," 24.
18. Steven S. Roberts, "Will 1992 Be the Year of the Woman?" *U.S. News & World Report* 112 (April 27, 1992): 37.
19. Ibid.
20. Alex S. Jones, "State Legislator Seeks Hill's Ouster," *New York Times*, October 16, 1991, A21.
21. Gwen Ifill, "Women See Champion In Law Professor," *New York Times*, November 17, 1991, 28.

3. *THE COST OF SEXUAL HARASSMENT*

1. Nancy Gibbs, "Office Crimes," *Time* 138 (October 21, 1991): 53.
2. Barbara Kantrowitz, "Striking a Nerve," *Newsweek* 118 (October 21, 1991): 37.
3. Ted Gest and Amy Saltzman, "Harassment: Men on Trial, *U.S. News & World Report* 111 (October 21, 1991): 30.
4. Ibid.
5. Dorothy Rabinowitz, "A Cautionary Tale: The High Price of a Wall Street Romance," *New York Magazine* 23 (January 8, 1990): 38.
6. Ibid.
7. Ibid.
8. Ibid.
9. Stephanie Strom, "Harassment Rules Often Not Pushed," *New York Times*, October 20, 1991, 1.
10. Brian S. Moskel, "Sexual Harassment '80s Style," *Industry Week* 238 (July 3, 1989): 22.
11. Catherine Breslin and Michelle Morris, "Please Leave Me Alone," *Working Woman* 13 (December 1988): 82.
12. Strom, "Harassment Rules," 2.
13. Ibid.
14. Ibid.

15. Jerry Buckley, "Watershed? Not Quite," *U.S. News & World Report* 111 (October 28, 1991): 40.

4. SEXUAL HARASSMENT IN SCHOOLS

1. "Donahue" #3445 (April 14, 1992).
2. Ibid.
3. Ibid.
4. Jane Gross, "Schools Are the Newest Arena for Sex Harassment Cases," *New York Times*, March 11, 1992, B8.
5. "Donahue."
6. Ibid.
7. Mark Walsh, "The Issue of Sexual Harassment in Schools Moves to Supreme Court," *Education Week* 10 (December 11, 1991): 15.
8. Gross, "Schools Newest Arena," B8.
9. Joan Roberts, "Women's Right to Choose, or Men's Right to Dominate," *Women in Higher Education*, ed. W. Todd Furniss and Patricia Graham (Washington, D.C.: American Council on Education, 1974), 51.
10. Frank J. Till, *Sexual Harassment: A Report on the Sexual Harassment of Students* (Washington, D.C.: Report of the National Advisory Council on Women's Educational Programs, 1980), 26–27.
11. Billie Wright Dziech and Linda Weiner, *The Lecherous Professor: Sexual Harassment on Campus* (Boston: Beacon Press, 1984), 78.
12. Ibid., 23.

5. WHAT YOU CAN DO

1. Linda Lynton, "The Dilemma of Sexual Harassment," *Sales and Marketing Management* 141 (October 1989): 68.
2. Vincent Bozzi, "Harassment Charges: Who Wins?" *Psychology Today* 23 (May 1989): 10.
3. Tamar Lewin, "Feminists Wonder if It Was Progress to Become 'Victims,' " *New York Times*, May 10, 1992, 6.

Index

abortion, 22
Abraham, Kathy, 32–35
Alliance for Justice, 14
American Association of University Professors, 54
American Council on Education, 49
Amherst Regional High School, 47
Aron, Nan, 14
Association for the Sexually Harassed (ASH), 31
Association of American Colleges' Project on the Status of Education of Women, 54–55
AT&T, 38, 39

Babineau, Mark, 1–2
Baker, Douglas, 61
Barnes, Paulette, 5
Barry, Patricia J., 8
Bates, Jim, 20
Bone, Mike, 2
Boston University, 7
Brown, Janet, 12–13
Browne-Allison, Lindsay, 29
Brown University, 56
Bush, George, 14

California, 10
California, University of, 17
California Women's Law Center, 3, 7
Central High (Duluth), 43
Civil Rights Act of 1964, 8
  Title VII of, 5, 69, 70
  Title IX of, 42
Civil Rights Act of 1991, 9–10, 70
Clerkin, Melissa, 29
Columbia-Barnard Task Force against Sexual Coercion, 54
Congress, U.S., 3
  as exempt from antidiscrimination laws, 20
  women in, 22–23
  see also Senate, U.S.
Conley, Frances, 58–59
consent, in teacher/student relationships, 50, 53–54
Corning, Inc., 38, 39
Court of Appeals, District of Columbia, 5
Crisp, Wendy, 27–28

day-care, 22
Democratic party, U.S., 14, 18, 21–22, 23–24

89

Democratic Senatorial Campaign Committee, 22
Doggett, John, 19
Du Pont, 38–39

Education Department, U.S., 14, 16
elephant walk, 55
Equal Employment Opportunity Commission (EEOC), U.S., 7, 10–11, 61
　offices of, 71–75
　"right-to-sue" letter from, 11
　settlements by, 10
　Thomas as head of, 12, 13, 14, 16, 18, 19
Estrich, Susan, 20

Faludi, Susan, 4–5
feminists, 4–5, 6–7, 66–67
　court decisions as viewed by, 9, 43
　in Japan, 25
　sexual harassment in schools as viewed by, 43, 47–48
　Thomas hearings and, 18, 20, 21–22, 25
Franklin, Christine, 41–43
Fund of the Feminist Majority, 22

Geffen Records, 1–2
Gomez-Preston, Cheryl, 29–31
graffiti, 43–44
Grossman, Frances, 7

Harris, Laurie, 2
Harvard Business Review, 48

Hill, Anita, 12–25
　in aftermath of hearings, 24–25
　as assistant to Thomas, 14, 15, 16, 18, 19
　background of, 13–14
　Specter's questioning of, 18–19, 23
　testimony of, 15–17, 20
　see also Thomas hearings
Holtzman, Ellen B., 9
Holy Cross College, 13
homosexuals, 4
"hostile environment" standard, 5, 6, 11, 44
House Ethics Committee, 20
Human Resources Department, Illinois, 61

Idaho, University of, 61
Internal Revenue Service (IRS), 6
Ireland, Patricia, 22
Island Records, 2

Japan, 25
Justice Department, U.S., 13

Kidd, Patricia, 26–27
Kouri, Karen, 8–9

lawsuits, *see* sexual harassment lawsuits
legislation, employee rights and, 69–70
　see also Civil Rights Act of 1964; Civil Rights Act of 1991
lesbians, 4

Liebman, Abby, 3
Long Dong Silver, 16
Lyle, Katy, 43–45

Marshall, Susan, 4
"mixed signals" claim, 8–9
Monohan, Linda, 35–36
Muck, Penny, 1–2
music business, 1–3

National Association for Female Executives, 28
National Association for the Advancement of Colored People (NAACP), 14
National Association for the Professional Saleswoman, 60
National Organization for Women, 22
Newsweek, 3
North Gwinnett High School, 41

Office of Civil Rights, 42
Oklahoma, University of, 14, 19, 24
Oklahoma State University, 13–14
Oral Roberts University, 14

Penthouse, 9
police officers, women as, 29–31

racism, 30, 38
rape, 6, 7
RCA, 2
"reasonable woman" standard, 6, 11

Republican party, U.S., 18, 23, 24
Resnick, Judith, 17
Rhode Island, University of, 49
Rozzi, Doris, 12

schools, sexual harassment in, 4, 41–59
  in colleges, 49–58
  in junior high and high schools, 41–49, 50, 54, 55, 57
  networking and, 66
  by peers, 43–44, 45–46, 48, 54–56
  policies on, 45, 46–48, 54, 57–58, 60–61, 62, 67
  in postgraduate programs, 58–59
  reporting of, 42, 43–44, 45–46, 47, 49–50, 56, 57
  by teachers, 41–42, 49–54, 57
Senate, U.S.:
  female staffers of, 20–21
  Thomas confirmed by, 19, 22
Senate Judiciary Committee, 12, 13, 14
  Hill questioned by, 18–19, 23
  Hill's testimony to, 15–17, 20
  Thomas's testimony to, 17
  see also Thomas hearings
sexual harassment:
  alcohol and, 64
  and being "one of the boys," 64–65
  as campaign issue, 22–23, 67
  defining of, 4, 38, 47, 54
  and direct confrontation of offender, 62–63

sexual harassment (*cont'd*)
  graffiti as, 43–44
  guidelines and tactics for victims of, 60–68
  in home, 6
  humor as tactic in confrontation of, 63
  instincts as defense against, 66
  leaving scene of, 64–65
  and maintenance of professional boundaries, 65–66
  men as victims of, 3–4
  men's views on, 6, 29, 30–31, 37, 67
  networking and, 66
  obscene jokes as, 4, 7
  and offender's exploitation of compassion, 65
  organizations concerned with, 77–79
  prevalence of, 3, 4–5, 6–7
  recording incidents of, 60
  same-sex victims of, 4
  in schools, *see* schools, sexual harassment in
  state laws on, 8, 10, 35, 44
  statistics on, 3, 5, 10–11, 36, 48, 49, 61
  on streets, 7
  stress associated with, 16, 27–28, 29, 31
  varieties of, 4, 5–6
  women blamed for, 8–9, 19
  in workplace, *see* workplace, sexual harassment in
sexual harassment lawsuits, 5–11
  aftermath of, 27–28, 29, 34–35
  attorneys' views on, 8, 9, 11, 61
  business responses to, 35–40
  ceiling on damages in, 9–10, 11
  comprehensive guidelines lacking in, 5, 11
  difficulties of proof in, 7–8, 60–61
  EEOC and, 10–11
  expert witnesses in, 10
  factors for success in, 61–62
  feminists' views on, 9, 43
  "hostile environment" standard in, 6, 11
  "mixed signals" claim in, 8–9
  policies as deterrent to, 47–48
  punitive damages awarded in, 8, 9–10, 11
  "reasonable woman" standard in, 6, 11
Smeal, Eleanor, 22
Southern California, University of, 20
Specter, Arlen, 18–19, 23
Stanford University School of Medicine, 58–59
Sullivan, Leonard E., 24
Supreme Court, U.S., 8, 40, 43, 44
  "hostile environment" ruling of, 6
  Thomas nominated to, *see* Thomas hearings

Tempstra, David, 61, 62
Texas, 10
Texas, University of, 4

Thomas, Clarence, 12–25, 43
  conservative views on, 12, 14
  as EEOC head, 12, 13, 14, 16, 18, 19
  Hill as assistant to, 14, 15, 16, 18, 19
  pornography and, 13, 15–16
  Senate confirmation of, 19, 22
  testimony of, 17
Thomas hearings, 12–25
  feminists' views on, 18, 20, 21–22, 25
  Hill's testimony in, 15–17, 20
  Thomas's testimony in, 17
  women in politics affected by, 22–24
Thoresen, Marjorie, 9
Thornburgh, Richard, 23
Townsend, Eliza, 23

U.S. News & World Report, 22

Van Halen, 3
Vinson, Mechelle, 5–6, 8

Washington State University, 61
Weinstock, Michael, 42

Women's Bar Association of the State of New York, 9
Women's Campaign Fund, 23
Woods, Harriet, 20
workplace, sexual harassment in, 1–3, 6, 8–10, 24, 26–40, 41, 60
  in blue-collar industries, 4–5
  as economic intimidation, 24, 28
  employee rights legislation and, 69–70
  in police departments, 29–31
  policies on, 35–40, 60–61, 62, 67
  reporting of, 27, 30–31, 34–35, 38–39
  stress associated with, 16, 27–28, 29, 31
  substantial court awards as deterrent to, 35–36
  victim criticized for, 27, 28–29, 30–31
  victim's silence about, 21, 28
  in Wall Street firm, 31–35
World Wrestling Federation, 4

Yale Law School, 13, 14, 19
Yeakel, Lynn, 23

Zeitz, Baila, 39